OLD PHILADELPHIA HOUSES
on Society Hill, 1750–1840

The Meredith house, 700 South Washington Square

Old
Philadelphia Houses
ON SOCIETY HILL, 1750–1840

ELIZABETH B. McCALL

Photographs by Michael Maicher

ROWMAN & LITTLEFIELD

Lanham • Boulder • New York • London

This book is affectionately dedicated to
My grandchildren,
ELIZABETH MARIS McCALL, ROBERT CARTER McCALL,
MELANIE JOY McCALL AND CAROLYN BARTOW McCALL
with the hope that when they are older they will become interested in the
history of early Philadelphia in which their ancestors took such an active part

Published by Rowman & Littlefield
A wholly owned subsidiary of The Rowman & Littlefield Publishing Group, Inc.
4501 Forbes Boulevard, Suite 200, Lanham, Maryland 20706
www.rowman.com

16 Carlisle Street, London W1D 3BT, United Kingdom

British Library Cataloguing in Publication Information Available

Library of Congress Cataloging-in-Publication Data

The Architectural Book Publishing Co., Inc., edition of this book was previously catalogued
by the Library of Congress as follows:

McCall, Elizabeth B.
    Old Philadelphia houses on Society Hill, 1750–1840, by Elizabeth B. McCall. Photos.
by Michael Maicher.
        192 p. illus., map (on lining papers) 28 cm.
        1. Historic buildings—Pennsylvania—Philadelphia. 2. Architecture, Domestic—
Pennsylvania—Philadelphia. I. Title.
        NA7238.P5 M3   66018357

ISBN 978-1-4422-2771-2 (pbk. : alk. paper)
ISBN 978-1-4422-2772-9 (electronic)

∞™ The paper used in this publication meets the minimum requirements of American
National Standard for Information Sciences—Permanence of Paper for Printed Library
Materials, ANSI/NISO Z39.48-1992.

Printed in the United States of America

CONTENTS

FOREWORD AND ACKNOWLEDGMENTS

PHILADELPHIA is spending more than two billion dollars of private, city, state and federal funds in an urban-renewal program that has earned nationwide attention. One of the most interesting of all the sections of the city being restored is Society Hill — officially known as Washington Square East. Its original name, Society Hill, has nothing to do with "society" in the Biddle-Vanderbilt sense; it was derived from the Free Society of Traders which, granted a charter by William Penn in 1682, soon set up a warehouse and office on the west side of Front Street, near the south bank of Dock Creek.

This area, bounded on the north by Walnut Street, on the west by Eighth Street, by Lombard Street on the south and on the east by the proposed Delaware Expressway, is being restored by the Philadelphia City Planning Commission in cooperation with the Redevelopment Authority, the Old Philadelphia Development Corporation, other associations and resident and non-resident individuals. It contains more eighteenth-century and early-nineteenth-century houses than any other comparable area in the United States. Included are some eighteenth-century mansions, quaint row houses of the eighteenth and early nineteenth centuries, eighteenth-century churches, the Head House and Old Second Street market, the buildings of several historic insurance companies and the famous Pennsylvania Hospital.

I regret that limitations of space have forced me to omit many Society Hill houses from this book. It is impossible, really, to do justice to Society Hill within the bounds of a single volume.

For the benefit of those persons who wish to see the interiors of some of the houses which are closed to the public except on tours, I offer this list of organizations that usually conduct annual house tours: the Pennsylvania Hospital, the National Society of Colonial Dames in the Commonwealth of Pennsylvania, the Home Owners and Residents Association of Washington Square East, Old Pine Street Presbyterian Church, the University of Pennsylvania Hospital Antiques Show and the Jefferson Hospital. Information about the annual Society Hill Week may be obtained from the Convention and Visitors' Bureau, 16th Street and John F. Kennedy Boulevard, or at the Office of City Representative, City Hall.

I wish to acknowledge with gratitude the help of many persons and organizations. First, Ellen Taussig, an old friend and feature writer for the Buffalo *Evening News,* for suggesting both the subject of this book and the publisher who would be interested in it. My husband, Shirley C. McCall, for his help; and our sons, S. Carter McCall, Jr., and J. Bartow McCall, who have been constant inspirations to me. All those who gave me permission to visit their houses or institutions under their care, and those from whose writings I have quoted or gained information: Nicholas B. Wainwright, C. P. Beauchamp Jefferys, L. Arnold Nicholson, Robert T. Trump, Dr. Margaret B. Tinkcom, the Rev. John S. Daley, S.J., Georgetown University, the Rev. John H. Leitch, the Rev. Joseph Koci, Jr., the Rev. Arnold Purdie, D.D., Mrs. Henry Miller Watts, Nathaniel Burt, Joan Church Roberts, Mrs. Joseph L. Eastwick, Mrs. C. Jared Ingersoll, Lewis M. Robbins, Mrs. Joseph Carson, Richard Powell, the Redevelopment Authority, the Philadelphia City Planning Commission, the Philadelphia Historical Commission, the Old Philadelphia Development Corporation and the Historical Society of Pennsylvania. Catalogues of the Antiques Show of the Hospital of the University of Pennsylvania and the Chestnut Hill Branch of the Philadelphia Free Library System proved of great assistance.

Elizabeth B. McCall

Chestnut Hill, Philadelphia
May 1965

NOTES ON THE DESIGN AND ARCHITECTURAL DETAIL OF PHILADELPHIA ROW HOUSES, 1740-1850*

PART OF THE value of every house depends on its appearance, which is determined by architectural design and detail. The architecture of old houses in the Society Hill and Washington Square areas is considered so valuable that the City of Philadelphia has taken steps to protect and make use of it. Regulations require owners to restore the façades, or street fronts, of their properties to original appearance for their own benefit and for that of the whole community. Plans for the alteration and restoration of houses certified as "historic" must have the approval of the Philadelphia Historical Commission. All properties in these urban-renewal areas, whether "historic" or not, also are required to meet rehabilitation standards established by the Redevelopment Authority.

The succeeding pictures and text outline the design and architectural details that gave Philadelphia houses their distinction, and indicate the approximate periods in which they were employed.

The row house is a Philadelphia institution — a space-saving, economical family dwelling which made this America's largest "city of homes." The design came from England with the first settlers and the traditional building material was red brick. Other masonry has been used. Brownstone was fashionable for larger houses in Victorian times. But Philadelphians still prefer brick.

The kinds of bricks, and the manner in which they are laid up to form walls, have changed over the years. Doorways, windows,

*Compiled from material in the archives of the Philadelphia Historical Commission and published by the Old Philadelphia Development Corporation. Text by L. Arnold Nicholson; drawings by Penelope Hartshorne. Used by permission of the Old Philadelphia Development Corporation.

roofs, cornices and other exterior features have changed, too. These are the architectural details related to the age of the house which give it character and distinction when — *and only when* — they are properly combined.

The illustration shows how the façades changed from the earliest houses that have been preserved to those built just prior to the Civil War. The dates are the approximate time when the design was most used.

The gambrel roof on the two-and-a-half story house, 1700–1750, is found on many dwellings built in the first half of the eighteenth century. This roof with a break in its pitch allowed the use of short rafters and increased headroom in attics. The flat shed roof above the attic dormer also is typical of this early period, as are the heavy cornice projecting above the second-story windows and the pent eave above the first floor. Such small houses with either one or two windows on the first floor, and with a straight sloped roof and pitched or gabled dormer were popular for many years — even after 1800. The house that replaced them as a home for people of modest means was the three-story bandbox with one room on each floor, topped by a shed roof. Many still line the city's small streets and alleys.

The three-and-a-half story houses dated 1750–1800 and 1765–1800 also might have been built at earlier dates, and the smaller of the two illustrated sometimes was ornamented with a pent eave. The house on the right is simply a more elaborate, costly version of its smaller neighbor. Both are Georgian in design, which we call Colonial because it was the predominant style before the Revolution, during the reign of George III.

The heavy cornices and bold ornamentation from Colonial times began to change shortly before 1800, when the design we refer to as Federal took form. Architects and builders employed lighter, more sophisticated detail. The dimensions and the glass area in homes enlarged, as shown by the house dated 1790–1820. More delicately molded architraves, or trim, surrounded doors and windows. Fanlights had appeared much earlier in the more elaborate homes. They now became almost universal.

The house farthest right represents Philadelphia's row-house version of the Greek Revival. The arched doorway and rounded dormer are typical of that time, which popularized the marble steps and accented sills and lintels below and above windows — both to persist, with alterations, through the Victorian decades into the present century.

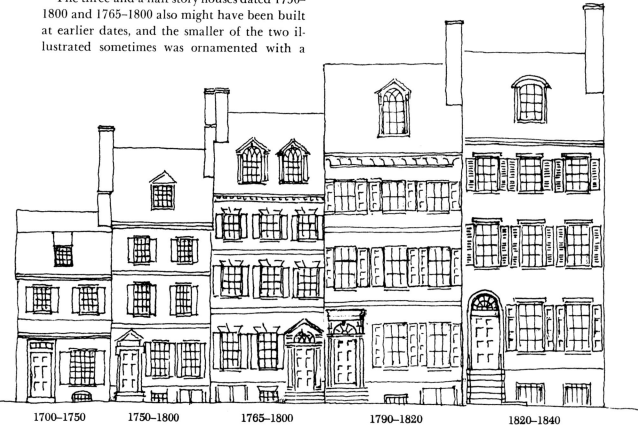

1700–1750   1750–1800   1765–1800   1790–1820   1820–1840

Walls of Brick

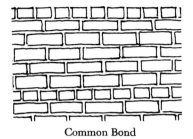

Common Bond

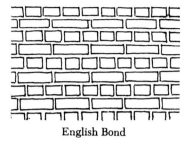

English Bond

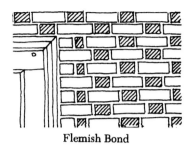

Flemish Bond

Brick was manufactured in and near Philadelphia from the beginning of settlement. The predominant color of well-burned local brick varies from a yellow pink to deep red, with the latter predominant. "Salmon brick" was an inexpensive, poorly burned type almost orange in color, usually used in party walls between houses. Flemish bond was most used for the façades of houses in the Colonial period, in which "headers" and "stretchers" alternate. A header is a brick laid across the wall to bind the two courses together, with its end exposed to the weather. Stretchers are laid with the long sides exposed. Glazed headers were often used in Flemish bond in Philadelphia, apparently for decorative effect. The glazed ends were produced by firing the brick to the point where the clay and sand fused to a bluish-black glassy surface. In common bond the custom today is to build a wall with a row of headers every seventh course. Eighteenth-century bricklayers, who often used common bond for rear walls, followed no set pattern. Header courses may have as few as three or as many as

Belt courses, located approximately at the floor level of upper stories, are a familiar architectural ornament in early Philadelphia houses. They add horizontal accents to the house, and were almost always built of brick in the Colonial period. The belt bricks sometimes were hand-rubbed to catch the light and usually were not glazed. Stone belt courses became popular after the Revolution. The illustrations show two types of brick construction and a stone belt course. Water tables serve a useful function by thickening the wall near ground

level. Brick water tables are found on all except the humblest dwellings built in the eighteenth century, and are simply a projecting course of brick beginning from the stone foundation to as much as four feet above the ground topped by a row of quarter-round bricks. Stone largely replaced the brick during the Federal period.

The mortar in use prior to 1850 did not contain cement. The mixture was lime and sand, and the color therefore depended on the color of the sand. The mortar joints between the bricks were struck with a hand tool (a) producing what is known as a grapevine joint (b). A simpler joint (c) frequently was used in back walls. The grapevine joint is not difficult for a mason equipped with the proper tool; modern substitutes for the old mortar can be made using lime with white instead of gray cement.

 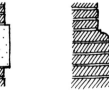

String or Belt Courses

Water Tables

ten stretcher courses between. English bond also was employed, and frequently appears in water tables at the base of a Flemish bond wall. Common bond replaced the more expensive Flemish on façades in the nineteenth century.

Cornices

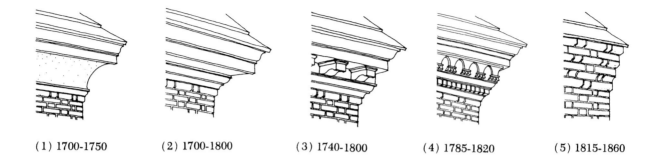

(1) 1700-1750   (2) 1700-1800   (3) 1740-1800   (4) 1785-1820   (5) 1815-1860

The cornice of an old house often offers the best clue to its age since it is least likely to have been drastically changed. Some small houses in the first half of the eighteenth century, and occasionally later, were built with a plaster cove cornice (1). The wood cornice also was employed and became almost universal after 1750 (2). Larger houses were ornamented with decorative brackets known as modillions on the cornices (3), sometime with dentils, or wooden "teeth," below, as shown in (4). The heavy modillions became more delicate prior to 1800. Decorations of classical origin were applied in low relief as cornices became lighter in the Federal period. A typical late Federal cornice is shown in (4). The brick cornice first appeared about 1815 (5).

Pent eaves were a protective cornice overhanging the windows and doorway of the first story, extending the full width of the facade. They were seldom built after 1770. One type, often matching the roof cornice above, was constructed with a plaster cove. The German settlers preferred a shed-type pent eave for their "suburban" homes in Germantown and it was also used on Philadelphia row houses. The illustrations show both types.

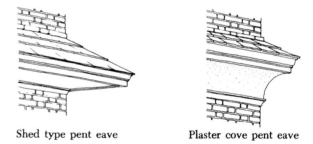

Shed type pent eave   Plaster cove pent eave

Doorways

The doorway into a row house offered the early builder an opportunity for ornamental design. The treatment depended on the wealth and inclination of the owner. The simplest arrangement was a plank-front frame to match the frames in the windows, topped by a four-light transom (1). A door with six raised panels was standard. Slightly more elaborate entranceways often employed an A-shaped pediment supported by brackets above the door trim, rising from a stone or marble stoop (2). The fanlight, at this period, was an innovation limited to the wealthy. The pediment and open pilasters were a less ornate, lighter treatment frequently used after the Revolution (3) when fanlights also became more widely used. The fanlight in an arched brick doorway began with the Federal period and carried through the first half of the nineteenth century (4). Note that the doors in (2) and (3), like that in (1), have panels raised flush with the stiles and rails. The door in (4) has recessed panels, bordered by applied molding. See Y-Y and z-z.

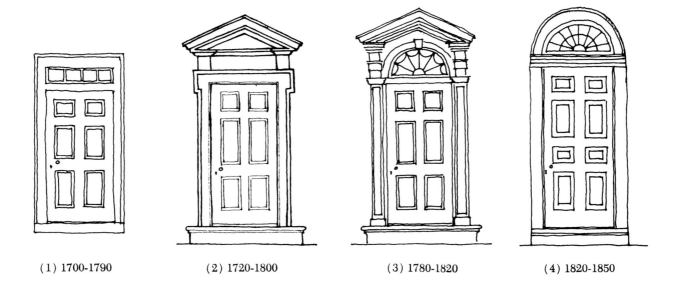

(1) 1700-1790   (2) 1720-1800   (3) 1780-1820   (4) 1820-1850

Windows and Shutters

The openings in the walls for windows, and the wood frames and sash set in them, subtly changed between 1750 and 1850. Hung sash, which remains the most popular to this day, was used. Only the bottom sash is moveable, however, in these early windows. A segmented brick arch was frequently used above the windows in the earliest dwellings (1). The wood frame set in the opening below is known as a plank-front, due to the wide surface that is exposed. The frame is set almost flush with the outside wall. Sills are flush or project slightly and usually were finished by the addition of a projecting show sill. Plank-front frames were cut from solid pieces of timber, mortised and pegged at the corners. These heavy boxlike enclosures apparently were considered strong enough to support the brick wall above and as time went on an arch was seldom used (2). Keystones, however, were frequently placed above windows for decoration in the larger dwellings. The plank-front window remained popular for many years, and is often found in the rear of houses where newer types appear in the front façade.

(1) 1700-1750

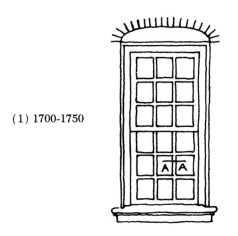

(2) 1750-1800

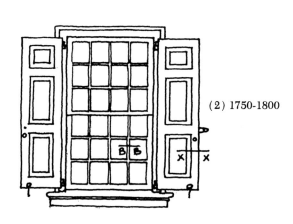

(3) 1790-1830

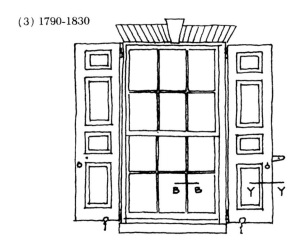

(4) 1820-1850

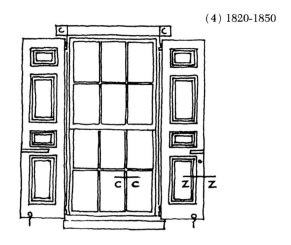

The beginning of the Federal period brought a new type of frame, known as reveal, which was recessed in the wall and eliminated the heavy appearance of the plank. The size of the panes of glass was increased at the same time, and the wood mullions holding the glass in the sash were narrowed. The splayed brick arch was popular (3). Refinement continued throughout the first half of the nineteenth century (4), and heavily accented stone lintels and sills appeared with the use of Greek Revival trim.

The shutters show similar change. The three-panel shutter (2) was most used all through the eighteenth century. The panels are raised flush with the stiles and rails that surround them (see section x-x and y-y). Shutters on larger houses often were of four-panel design (3). The raised panels were replaced by depressed panels (4) ornamented by applied moldings (z-z) late in the Federal period and thereafter. Note that the fasteners for shutters are on a rail or crosspiece between panels, which is below the top of the lower sash. Louvered instead of solid shutters also were used throughout the nineteenth century. Interior shutters are found in houses of all periods.

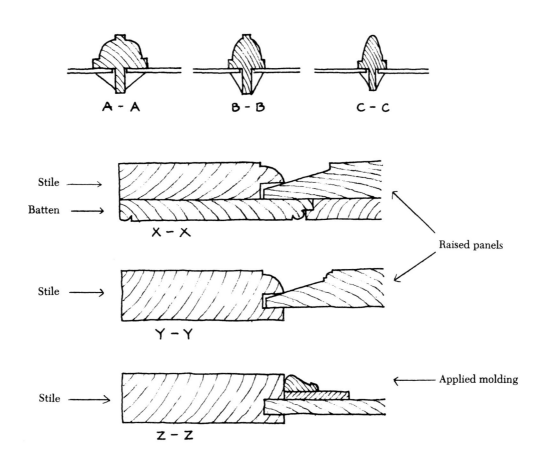

Cross-sections of mullions (top) and shutters (below) on opposite page.

Hardware

The hardware on the façades of old houses is one of the many little details which are important. The placement of the knob in a front door, for instance, is determined by the type of latch and lock inside. Box locks were used in Georgian and Federal dwellings, placing the knob four or more inches from the edge of the door, in a position quite different from that required by more modern locks mortised into the door.

Shutters were hung on offset strap hinges, pivoted on iron pins, or pintles, near the top and bottom of window frames. The pintles on Colonial plank-front frames were known as "drive" pintles, since they were attached to a spike driven into the solid wood frame. On later reveal frames the supports for the pintles are either wedged between the frame and the brick or screwed to the frame.

The fastening device most used for shutters in the eighteenth century has a small metal rod which goes through the hole in the other shutter at (A) and is fastened with a pin on the inside. Slide bolts became more popular after the Revolution.

"Dogs" to hold open shutters flat against the wall were made in a variety of designs. The simplest, and most used in the eighteenth century, is shown. More elaborate designs were used later in the nineteenth century.

Strap hinges were used on cellar bulkhead doors, pivoted on pintles set in the stone cheeks, or sidepieces. The fastener illustrated was the most popular in Georgian and Federal periods.

OLD PHILADELPHIA HOUSES
on Society Hill, 1750–1840

The Barclay house, 217 Delancey Street, built 1756-1758 for Alexander Barclay, comptroller of the Port of Philadelphia.

THE BARCLAY HOUSE

A Statue of Neptune on a seahorse found in ruins near Rome is the main feature of the attractive garden behind the Barclay House. The statue is surrounded by flowering shrubs and trees.

The Barclay House, 217 Delancey Street, built between 1756 and 1758 for Alexander Barclay, Comptroller of the Port of Philadelphia under George II and George III, has been purchased by Mr. and Mrs. F. Otto Haas, of Ambler, Pennsylvania. It is being restored for them by Robert T. Trump — unfortunately, not in time to have the interior photographed for this book.

Samuel Rhoads, builder of the Barclay House, also built Benjamin Franklin's house, no longer standing, and the original east wing of the Pennsylvania Hospital. The house, of brick with a pent eave and a modillion cornice, has a gambrel roof common in the first half of the eighteenth century. There are bull's-eye lights above the front door, which has original HL hinges and a great iron lock. The front hall has a finely designed pedimented arched doorway above the entrance to the parlor. In the parlor there is an original paneled wooden chimney breast with fireplace facings of gray King of Prussia marble. A deep wood cornice, paneled wainscoting and random-width pitch-pine flooring are other features. There is an elegant large old brass lock with a drop handle on the door. The staircase is the finest known example in a mid-eighteenth-century Philadelphia private house.

The dining room looks out on a garden decorated with a marble Renaissance fountain of Neptune on a seahorse, discovered in ruins near Rome and previously in the Louis Duhring collection. It is appropriate, for the house's original owner was interested in the sea and shipping.

In the basement is the oldest original wine cellar in Society Hill, with a stone shelf for holding a candle. There is a modern kitchen.

The second-floor master bedroom has original eighteenth-century Delft tiles facing the fireplace. There is an additional bedroom and bath, and the third floor also has two bedrooms and a bath.

Bell's Court, Orianna Street, in the rear of 221 South Fourth, built between 1813 and 1815, originally consisted of eight small houses, only four of which have survived.

BELL'S COURT

Bell's Court — so named because two merchants, William Bell and Robert Bell, once lived there — on Orianna Street, in the rear of 271 South Fourth Street, was built between 1813 and 1815. It originally consisted of eight small houses but there are now only four. These were restored about 1960 by Robert T. Trump, who purchased them from the Redevelopment Authority.

The four houses make a charming group. Each one has an eleven-by-fourteen living room, a basement that combines dining room and kitchen, and two nine-by-eleven bedrooms, one above the other, with baths added. They are of red brick with white trim, and there are dark green doors and shutters, half-gambrel roofs and dentil cornices. The court has been attractively fenced and planted.

The houses are not open to the public except on house tours, and then only the front doors are open, as the buildings are too small to permit much pedestrian traffic. Those wishing to see the court should go north on Third Street, turn west on Willing's Alley and south on Orianna. The court is on the right.

The Bouvier houses, at 258, 260 and 262 South Third Street, were built between 1830 and 1839. Michel Bouvier, great-great-grandfather of Mrs. John F. Kennedy, bought them in 1849.

THE BOUVIER HOUSES

Ebony inlaid desk made by Michel Bouvier, in the parlor of the Bouvier house being restored by Mr. and Mrs. James C. Crumlish, Jr.

Believed to be the only brownstone-front houses in Society Hill, the Bouvier Houses — so called because Michel Bouvier, great-great grandfather of Mrs. John F. Kennedy, once owned them — are at Nos. 258, 260 and 262 South Third Street. The three houses are similar but not identical. I have been in No. 262, now occupied and being restored by former District Attorney James C. Crumlish, Jr., and Mrs. Crumlish. The other two are currently rooming houses but have been purchased by individuals who plan to restore them.

The site of the three houses was occupied in 1809 by William Bingham, whose house was considered to be one of the most elegant in Philadelphia, if not in the entire country. Later it became the Washington Benevolent Society, where Lafayette once attended a banquet for William Rush, United States Minister to the Court of St. James. The society's building was destroyed by fire on St. Patrick's Day, 1823, and in 1830 the three brownstone fronts were erected in its place.

In 1849 Michel Bouvier, mahogany and marble merchant, purchased the properties, made the middle one his home and rented out

the other two. Other well known persons who lived there were Thomas Cadwalader, Thomas Mayne Willing, Charles Willing Hare and Dr. David Jayne. At one time No. 262 was a convent and school for the Sisters of St. Joseph.

A survey made in 1871 describes Nos. 258 and 260 as "brownstone with a brownstone balcony supported on four stone brackets with an iron railing thirty inches high, stone entablature over doors and windows, eight brackets under planeier [?] entablature and blocking course on consoles over each window on second and third stories."

The Crumlish house, an interesting example of Empire architecture, has a set of balustrades leading from the street to the main floor. The house has high ceilings, carved marble mantelpieces, ornamental cornices and decor on the ceilings. The front windows go down to the floor and have inside shutters. The walls are very thick, almost eliminating all street noises.

Mrs. Crumlish calls her house "one of the first split levels," the rooms in the rear being higher than those in front, a feature found in

Tall windows with elaborately carved window frames and inside shutters, Bouvier house, 262 South Third Street.

Marble Empire mantelpiece in the double parlor of the house once owned by Michel Bouvier, 262 South Third Street.

many old Philadelphia houses. On the ground floor there are a large double parlor with two marble fireplaces, a dining room and a modern kitchen — installed by the present owners. Halfway up in the rear is a former chapel, with stained-glass windows still in place — now a children's playroom — and further up there are an upstairs sitting room, large bedroom and bath facing the street. The next level has three bedrooms and a bath in the rear, and three more bedrooms in the front. The fourth floor, closed on account of the fire laws, contains two rooms.

Mrs. Crumlish, who picks up Empire pieces and has them done over for the house, is most proud of an ebony inlaid desk made by Michel Bouvier, who was a cabinetmaker. Elaborately done, it has a drawer lined in gold damask.

The house is not open to the public.

Finely carved door frame in the parlor of the Bouvier house, 262 South Third Street.

This elaborately carved gilt Empire mirror and small sofa are in the parlor of the Bouvier house, 262 South Third Street.

The front door of the Bracken house, an original, shows pilasters, pediment and fanlight. The door itself is a restoration. Small door at left is an entrance to an alley, typical of many Philadelphia houses.

28

The Bracken House

THE BRACKEN HOUSE

The Bracken house, 300 Delancey Street, is a brick row house, typical of the late eighteenth and early nineteenth centuries. It has an original dormer window, unusual cornice and door with pilasters and pediment. *Courtesy Mr. and Mrs. John P. Bracken.*

The house at 300 Delancey Street is a quaint example of a small early-nineteenth-century Philadelphia row house. It was built in 1806 on land acquired from the University of Pennsylvania in 1804. Mr. and Mrs. John P. Bracken bought the house in 1962 and it was restored by Charles E. Peterson and Edgar G. Cross, 2nd, architects, and Robert T. Trump, builder.

Built of brick in the Flemish bond style, it is three and a half stories high, with one room on each floor. The top floor has an original dormer window, in perfect condition. Belt courses of Schuylkill marble separate the first and second stories, and the second and third. The house has a fine, most unusual cornice, with modillions and dentils.

The original doorway, with fanlight and pediment, is typical of those built in the period 1765-1800. The marble steps and doorsill are original, but not the door itself. Bathrooms and a modern kitchen have been added.

The living room contains the original, beautifully carved mantelpiece, decorated with molded plaster. When the Brackens acquired the house, this mantelpiece was covered by ten or more coats of paint, the outermost being a bright red. The fireplace is faced with King of Prussia (Pennsylvania) marble, darker than that found in most old houses in the area.

In the basement, the east-west supports for either side of the house are brick arches, a feature of all the old houses on this side of Delancey Street's 300 block. The central arch in the south side has been fitted up as a fireplace, with many old kitchen utensils, some of which were found in the house.

Filled with potted plants or flowers as the season permits, the tiny garden which Mrs. Bracken has made behind the living room offers a charming vista through a Thomas Jefferson window (not original). The house is open to the public only during house tours.

The central arch of the three forming the basement support of the Bracken house has been made into a fireplace with old fittings, some of which were found in the house.

The Bracken House

This view of the Bracken house shows the original dormer window and the unusual cornice with modillions and dentils. The fire mark is that of the Green Tree, the Mutual Assurance Company founded in 1784.

The Bracken House

The original fireplace in the living room of the Bracken house, 300 Delancey Street, faced with King of Prussia marble, is handsomely carved in wood and molded in plaster.

The Bracken House

Vista through Bracken house living-room windows shows a tiny garden filled with potted plants and flowers. The Thomas Jefferson window is not original.

The Carson houses, 704 and 706 South Washington Square.

THE CARSON HOUSES

View of railing and front door, Carson house.

The Carson houses, 704 and 706 South Washington Square, are two of the few that remain of those that once surrounded the square in which are buried 2000 American soldiers who died in the Revolution. Most of the buildings bordering the square today are occupied by publishing concerns and other businesses and a high-rise apartment.

Built in 1816, the Carson houses are Federal with Georgian characteristics. They are of brick, with fanlights above the doors. Double white-marble steps with graceful wrought-iron railings converge on either side before the two front doors. There are high ceilings, tall windows, very thick walls and inside shutters. There are six handsome mantelpieces, of carved dark-gray Chester County marble. The one in the living room is Tuscan, that in the library Ionic and the one in the dining room, Doric.

Before the Carsons bought the houses in 1959 to restore them, they had been made into twenty-one studios. One of the studios, used as

a hideaway by Christopher Morley, the writer, is now the Carson library.

Mrs. Carson, whose main dwelling is at No. 706, has made a cut through into No. 704 on the second-floor front, so that large dining and living rooms now look out onto the square. Here she has a rare collection of furniture, most of which belonged to the late Mr. Carson's ancestors.

This eighteenth-century Philadelphia furniture rivals that found in many museums. The pieces include an asymmetrical gilt mirror, Chippendale chairs, some with the claw-and-ball feet, others with trifid or shod trifid feet. There are three lowboys, a Chippendale chest, a Thomas Morton clock, a rare hanging cabinet and a magnificent highboy. The dining-room chairs are Sheraton. Mrs. Carson also has a handsome collection of Lowestoft or Chinese export china.

The Carson houses are not open to the public.

Carson house fireplace.

A portrait of Dr. Joseph Carson, an ancestor, hangs above the gray Chester County marble mantelpiece in the home of Mrs. Joseph Carson.

An unusual eighteenth-century asymmetrical gilt mirror hangs above the sofa in the parlor of the home of Mrs. Joseph Carson.

OVERLEAF: A view of the parlor at the Carson house, showing Chippendale chairs and a large Lowestoft or Chinese bowl on table. Beyond is the dining room.

This view of a corner of the Mrs. Joseph Carson home, 706 South Washington Square, shows a handsome highboy and, to the left, a Philadelphia Chippendale chest and chair. The clock is by Thomas Morton.

THE DILWORTH HOUSE

The Dilworth House, on East Washington Square between the buildings of The Athenaeum and J. B. Lippincott, publishers, is a copy of a colonial home. Designed by G. Edwin Brumbaugh, architect, it was built in 1957 by John S. Cornell.

When Mr. and Mrs. Richardson Dilworth bought two eighteenth-century houses at this location, the architect and the builder decided the structures were not sturdy enough for restoration, as the salmon bricks were crumbling and the walls were buckling. Much to the regret of everyone, the decision was made to tear down the two old houses and build a copy, as Mr. and Mrs. Henry Miller Watts did on Spruce Street.

The result was a most attractive three-and-a-half story red-brick Colonial house, with white trim. It has a door with Doric columns and a pediment, white-marble belt courses between the floors, marble-splayed brick arches above the windows, a dentil cornice and a slate roof.

The Dilworth house, East Washington Square. The Green Tree fire mark may be seen on the third floor.

42

FACING PAGE: The Drinker house, 241 Pine Street, is an early Philadelphia house of red brick with a pent eave, plain cornice, dormer window, simple door and brick belt course between second and third floors.

Detail of front door and portal, Dilworth house.

A wrought-iron fence at the side and a large garden in the rear embellish the house, the interior of which is furnished with antiques inherited by Mrs. Dilworth from her grandmother.

Mr. Dilworth, a former mayor of Philadelphia, is a prominent lawyer, a partner in Dilworth, Paxson, Kalish and Dilks. Currently serving as chairman of a special committee set up to study rapid transportation between Boston and Washington, Mr. Dilworth also recently was made president of the Philadelphia School Board.

The Dilworths have felt compelled to close the interior of their house to photographers and to house tours, although it was open to the Pennsylvania Hospital tour for some five years. There were so many requests to open the house and such crowds streamed through it that Mrs. Dilworth finally found it impossible to cope with the problem. Many people thought that since it was the mayor's house it must be public property and open to sightseers. However, it was not an official residence but was built by the Dilworths as their personal home, at their own expense.

The Dilworth House

THE DRINKER HOUSE and DRINKER'S COURT

The Drinker House, 241 Pine Street, stands on land that once was part of a grant made by William Penn to the Free Society of Traders. Charles Brockden, who acquired it from the trustees of the Society, conveyed it to his son Richard in 1732. Richard devised the land to his daughter, Letitia Pryor, in 1754, and she sold it to John Drinker in 1765.

John Drinker, a brick mason and, later, a merchant and builder, erected the house before 1767. The Drinker family has been prominent in Philadelphia for three centuries. John Drinker's descendants today include Catherine Drinker Bowen, the biographer, and Ernesta Drinker Ballard, executive secretary of the Pennsylvania Horticultural Society and author of several books on growing plants and flowers.

The house, typical of the earliest Philadelphia brick houses, with Georgian doorway and pent eave, was restored in 1955 by L. Arnold Nicholson, a writer and former *Saturday Evening Post* editor, and Mrs. Nicholson. The Nicholsons were among the first to return to Society Hill.

The Nicholsons' house is almost completely original, with a living room that has a fireplace and paneled wall; above, a paneled master bedroom with a fireplace; and a similar room on the third floor, with a large attic. The paneling above the living-room fireplace has dog-ears that go into the cornice, an unusual feature. Side and back yards are planted with trees and shrubbery, and there is a brick-paved patio.

Drinker's Court, entered from Delancey Street behind the Drinker House, is notable for a main house, facing Delancey Street, that has just one room on each floor and is known as a "Father, Son and Holy Ghost" house. The Nicholsons have restored the four very small houses on the west side of the court and made them into apartments; they are known as bandbox houses. The Nicholsons also hope to buy and restore the houses on the east side of the court.

The Drinker House and Drinker's Court are open for house tours.

The Drinker House and Drinker's Court

Drinker's Court as seen from Delancey Street. One small house faces the street; the other four, which have been made into apartments, face on the court.

Corner cupboard, Drinker house dining room.

The Drinker House and Drinker's Court

Fireplace, Drinker house parlor.

The Drinker House and Drinker's Court 49

Drinker house master bedroom.

THE HEAD HOUSE

Head house and market. The Old Second Street Market, built in 1745, was restored in the late 1950s by the City of Philadelphia.

THE HEAD HOUSE and OLD MARKET

One of the most unusual and picturesque parts of Society Hill is the Head House (formerly a fire-engine house), along with the oldest part of the "New Market" behind it, at Second and Pine streets.

The original market, built in 1745, was restored by the City of Philadelphia in the early 1960s. The Head House, built in 1804, was restored at the same time. The market once extended south to Cedar Street (now South Street), where there was another firehouse. The latter building and that part of the market from Lombard to South Street were gone by 1860.

The Head House, used for fire apparatus in the old days of the volunteer fire companies, for many years housed the equipment of the Fellowship and Hope companies. An attractive early-nineteenth-century building of red brick with white trim and green shutters and doors, it is surmounted by a white cupola that once contained a fire bell. Citizens of the "lower district" of the city raised money for the bell as well as a clock. Two stories high and, according to specifications published in 1804 in the *American Daily Advertiser*, designed to hold "two fire engines with their apparatus," the Head House is bisected by an archway to the market.

A large room with closets on the second floor was for the use of the fire companies. It is said that some market business was conducted there too. Machinery for the clock is above. The Head House today contains an antique hose reel on loan from the collection of the Insurance Company of North America, in the west building. The house to the east is currently occupied by Captain Cavenaugh, a retired fireman.

In 1802, before the final extension of the market north to Pine Street, there were sixty-eight permanent stalls and thirty-three extra wooden ones in the area now to the rear of the Head House. The market shed consists of brick piers supporting a gabled roof above an arched, plastered ceiling, like those in some markets in rural England and the Low Countries. The permanent stalls were in the market shed, then called the "shambles." An 1829 visitor from Natchez described the market as having "a profusion of meats and vegetables of the finest kind" and added that "Philadelphia beef is unrivalled in the world."

Although a city undertaking, the old Second Street Market was privately financed, and for twenty-five years Joseph Wharton, a wealthy merchant and landowner, and Mayor Edward

Old Market and Head house. BELOW: Information booth built by the City of Philadelphia. Head house and market may be seen to the rear.

Early nineteenth-century hose reel in Head house.

Shippen collected the rents in lieu of interest on their original capital outlay. When the city decided to take over the market in 1772, Wharton demanded sixty-four pounds in reimbursement (whether he ever received it is not known). In 1795 the City Council recommended extension of the market to South Street; and in 1804 it was extended north to Pine.

Market days were Tuesdays and Fridays, daylight to two P.M. from April first to September first, and daylight to three P.M. in the winter. In 1800 sellers of fresh and salted fish were required to "stand in a single row on each side of the market," beginning at Pine Street. Vendors of roots, herbs and vegetables and of fruit and garden seed occupied the stands under the eaves on the east side. Those offering butter and eggs for sale took their places under the eaves on the west side of the north shambles. Butchers were in the market house proper. Farmers coming from New Jersey with baskets and carts of produce could sell their wares from carts arranged along the curb without paying a fee. A stand under the eaves cost three pounds in Mr. Wharton's time. Rents went up in 1809, and by mid-century new trouble arrived as open-air markets lost their popularity.

Now it is planned to make the entire area a shopping center. A red-brick, shingle-roofed information center has been built on Second Street, and a once handsome old house at the southeast corner of Pine and Second will be an inn. Houses to the west of the market are being restored as shops.

G. Edwin Brumbaugh was the architect in charge of restoring the Market and Head House. The market may be seen at any time. Head House is open for various neighborhood church and hospital benefits. Permission to go inside at other times may be secured by telephoning Captain Cavenaugh (MU6-4589).

The Head House and Old Market

This doorway at 321 South Fourth Street is now boarded up as the Hill-Physick-Keith house awaits a restorer. Picture taken in 1911. *Courtesy Philadelphia Historical Commission.*

THE HILL-PHYSICK-KEITH HOUSE

The Hill-Physick-Keith House, 321 South Fourth Street, was purchased in May 1965 by the Philadelphia Society for the Preservation of Landmarks through a grant made by the Annenberg Fund. The Fund, which is headed by Walter H. Annenberg, publisher of the *Philadelphia Inquirer,* has made a further grant to be used in restoring the mansion, one of the handsomest and certainly the largest Colonial house left in Society Hill.

The house, of nine-inch red-brick walls, has three stories and an attic, with four dormer windows and a shingled hip roof. Besides the thirty-two-room mansion there are a coach house, a stable with four stalls and a large brick-walled garden to the south.

On the first floor there are an entry with a marble tiled floor with molded marble sub-skirting, a staircase that has a mahogany rail with scrollwork at the bottom and fancy mahogany balusters. There are three parlors, two kitchens, a storeroom and a pantry. The main rooms have stucco cornices, yellow-pine floors, molded subskirting and architraves. There are two carved marble mantelpieces on the first floor.

The second floor has six rooms and two entries, with stucco cornices and five marble mantelpieces. On the third floor are five rooms and two entries, again with stucco cornices and, here, four mantelpieces of marble. The attic has four rooms and an entry.

The house is believed to have been built by Henry Hill, importer and wine merchant, in 1786. The rear seems to be of earlier construction than the front. Hill, a member of the City Troop, was a bachelor who gave many gay parties. It is said that during his occupancy the cellar contained a dungeon where Hill punished refractory seamen.

A later owner, James Vaux, sold the house in 1815 to Abigail Physick, spinster, for $30,-000. It was sold again in the same year to Dr. Philip Syng Physick, often known as the father of modern surgery, who for many years was associated with the Pennsylvania Hospital. Here, in 1824, Dr. Physick entertained for General Lafayette. And it was here that Chief Justice John Marshall, eighty years old and suffering a disease of the liver, came to consult Dr. Physick in 1835. Marshall died in Philadelphia, and it was while it was being tolled for his funeral procession that the Liberty Bell was cracked.

Carved cornice and ceiling decoration in southwest parlor, Hill-Physick-Keith house. *Courtesy Philadelphia Historical Commission.*

This picture of the home of Dr. Philip Syng Physick, "the father of modern surgery," was taken sometime before 1902. *Courtesy Philadelphia Historical Commission.*

The Hill-Physick-Keith House

The Hill-Physick-Keith house, 321 South Fourth Street, as it looked in 1965 before Philadelphia Society for the Preservation of Landmarks began restoration, scheduled for completion by 1968.

In 1838 the house became the property of Sarah E. Randolph, who left it to her son, Philip Syng Physick Randolph. In 1895, Randolph sold it, for $81,500, to Sarah Edyth Wister and her sister, Elsie Wister, who later married Charles Penrose Keith. Mrs. Keith died in 1935, leaving the house to the Pennsylvania Hospital. The Redevelopment Au-

thority secured it through condemnation in 1962.

George Brooke Roberts will be the architect for the restoration, which was started in the winter 1966 and will take at least two years to complete. It has been decided to restore the house in the style of the Federal period of 1815.

THE INGERSOLL HOUSE

One of the most popular stops on house tours today is the Ingersoll House, 217 Spruce Street. It was built in 1759 by Samuel Davis, who must have been a master builder although he called himself a "house carpenter."

The first survey made by the Philadelphia Contributionship in 1781 describes the house thus: "21.2 feet front including the alley 30 feet deep 9 inch party walls — plaster partitions — dog legg stairs with half paces — both storys painted — shingling about 22 years old — the kitchen 12 feet by 16 feet 2 stories high 9 inch walls. On the house three hundred pounds — kitchen one hundred pounds" (this indicating amount of insurance coverage). In those times the kitchen was sometimes a separate building, often attached to the house by a covered walkway.

Built of old brick, the house is three and a half stories high, with brick belt courses between the floors. The front door, typical of the period 1720-1800, is eight-paneled, with a pediment above. The half story contains a dormer window.

Mr. and Mrs. C. Jared Ingersoll, of Fort Washington, Pennsylvania, acquired the place in 1959 to use as a town house. It was a virtual shambles, occupied by squatters and infested with rats. The Ingersolls restored it lovingly, discerning in the wreck much of the original woodwork, fireplaces, chair rail and other features. While there had been nineteen previous owners the house had never been seriously damaged or altered. In some rooms eighteen coats of paint were scraped off before the original colors were revealed. The Ingersolls moved in in 1961.

The entire north wall of the master bedroom has all the original woodwork, including fireplace, overmantel and two chimney-breast closets. In the second-floor front drawing room, which also has all the original woodwork, is a fireplace with facings of Pennsylvania blue marble. This marble, the same as King of Prussia or Chester County marble, while called blue is really gray. The dining-room woodwork and the archway in the downstairs hall are likewise original.

The Ingersolls have embellished the house with eighteenth-century antiques, most of them heirlooms of Mr. Ingersoll's family. The entering visitor finds himself in a long, narrow hall,

The Ingersoll house, 217 Spruce Street.

Ingersoll house front door.

DAVIS-LENOX HOUSE
Built in 1759 by JAMES DAVIS
house carpenter & officer of
the Carpenters Company Added to
in 1784 by Major DAVID LENOX
continental soldier, 44th member
First City Troop, President of the
Bank of the U.S., U.S.Marshal
for the District of Pennsylvania,
Representative of the U.S. to
the Court of St. James.

to the left of which is the dining room, with an eighteenth-century English pedestal table. A Thomas Sully portrait of Alexander Wilcocks, brother of an earlier Mrs. Jared Ingersoll, hangs over an old Philadelphia card table. To the rear is a modern kitchen.

The master bedroom has in it an eighteenth-century ladder-back chair that belonged to the second owners of the house, Major and Mrs. David Lenox. Major Lenox was a member of the Light Horse of the City of Philadelphia and held many important positions, United States Representative to the Court of St. James, among others. His wife Tacy was a noted beauty. The Lenoxes added the third floor and garret and built a new kitchen.

The second-floor front drawing room contains a Sully portrait of Mrs. Jared Ingersoll, the former Miss Wilcocks and daughter-in-law of the Jared Ingersoll who was a signer of the Constitution. Here also are part of a set of mahogany Queen Anne chairs attributed to Savery and a collection of Lowestoft or Chinese export china.

FACING PAGE: Second-floor front living room, Ingersoll house, showing original woodwork, facings of Pennsylvania blue marble in fireplace and (right) a handsome Queen Anne mahogany armchair attributed to Savery.

Ingersoll house hall, showing original chair rail, archway and staircase.

The Ingersoll House

Master bedroom, Ingersoll house.

Ingersoll house dining room, showing damask curtains, eighteenth-century English pedestal table and some of the Ingersolls' antique china and silver.

FACING PAGE: The Latta house, 425 Spruce Street, of red brick with two belts of white marble, has an unusual cornice with carved swags below it.

Alexander Wilcocks portrait, Ingersoll dining room.

The Ingersoll House

THE LATTA HOUSE

The Latta house mantelpiece is early nineteenth-century Adams from an old house on Pine Street. The Rowlandson painting is flanked by French cache pots and vases with glass prisms.

THE LATTA HOUSE

Latta house cornice and original dormer window.

The Cuthbert H. Latta House, 425 Spruce Street, was built in 1792 by William Williams, builder of a number of houses in the Society Hill area. It was then occupied by Chalmers Moore Wharton, member of a prominent Philadelphia family that has taken an active part in the city's history. The house was re-modeled in 1834. When Mr. and Mrs. Latta bought it for restoration in 1963 it had fallen into disrepair and had become a rundown rooming house.

Built of brick, the three-and-a-half-story structure is noted for its unusual cornice, with modillions, dentils and a band of carving of swags and flowers. The entrance, typical of the 1820-1850 period, has fanlight above the door.

The Lattas have used Newport, Rhode Island, colors instead of the usual Williamsburg or Philadelphia colors on the inside. The living room is painted putty color, with putty gold on the woodwork. The original mantel-pieces having long since disappeared, the Lattas procured an early-nineteenth-century Adam mantel, from an old house on Pine Street, to use in their living room. Above is a Rowland-son painting, flanked by French cache pots and vases with glass prisms. The master bed-room has an early eighteenth-century mantel-piece taken from a house on Lombard Street. Twenty or more layers of paint had to be re-moved from the old mantelpieces to reveal their delicate carving.

The Lattas are enthusiastic clock collectors, and in the living room are three grandfather clocks, one made in Edinburgh by William Auld in 1810, another by Thomas Hargraves of England, the third by Solomon Yeakel, of Bucks County, Pennsylvania.

The graceful, curving staircase is a reproduc-tion, but the archways from the living room past the powder room and kitchen to the dining room and on the second floor are origi-nal. The downstairs arch is carved in wood, the second-floor arch in plaster.

The dining room is bordered on two sides by a small garden with a fountain, filled with evergreens and flowers in season. A late-seven-teenth-century Welsh dresser is filled with iron-stone china.

The Latta House, which was restored by Van Arkle and Moss, designers and builders, is open on house tours.

OVERLEAF: Latta house dining room, showing a seventeenth-century Welsh dresser filled with colorful eighteenth-century ironstone china. The clock was made by J. Richmond Bradford, early nineteenth century.

69

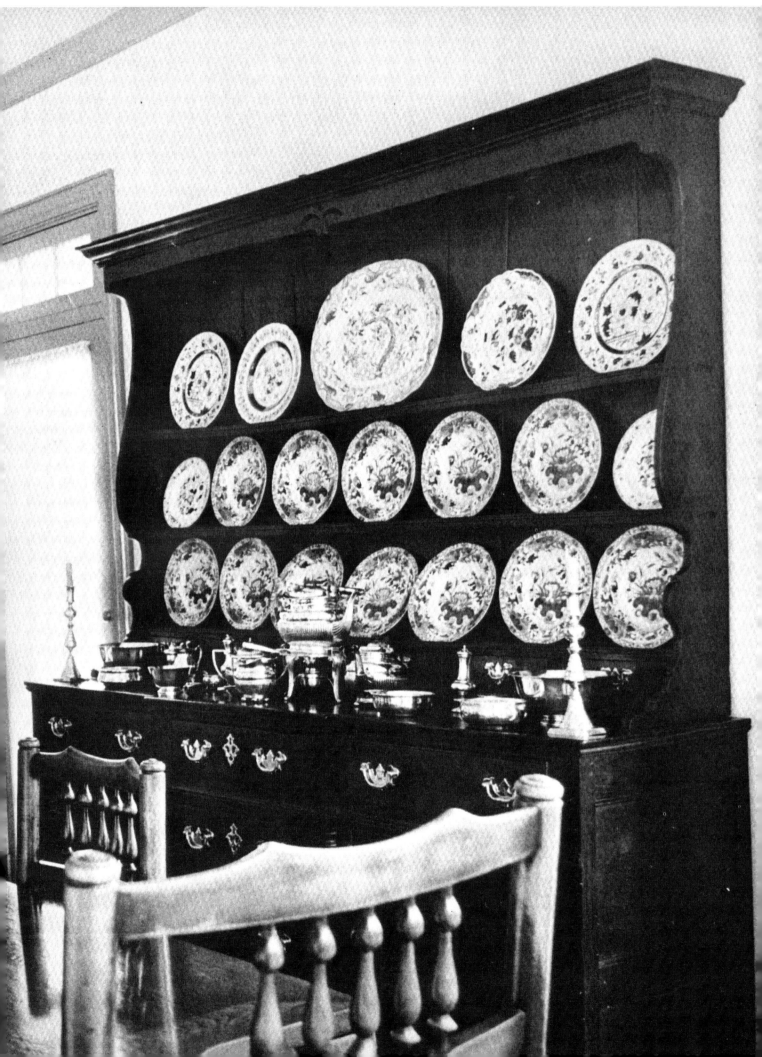

Left above, first-floor hall of Latta house, showing original archways. Right above, Latta house stairway. Right below, second-floor hall, showing original carving in archway.

Latta house, second-floor bedroom, showing mantelpiece taken from an old house on Lombard Street.

The Latta house garden is walled with brick and has a brick path edged with evergreens and flowers in season.

FACING PAGE: The Little house, 328 South Third Street, restored by Mr. and Mrs. Lewis M. Robbins, has a carved panel above the attractive fireplace.

74

Chippendale secretary in the parlor of the Little house.

An interesting little bedroom under the eaves on the third floor of the Little house.

The Little House, 328 South Third Street, was built in 1771 on land purchased from the Reverend Jacob Duché, rector of St. Peter's Church, who lived on the southeast corner of Third and Pine. Builder John Piles was a house carpenter and a member of the Carpenters Company, whose Carpenter Hall was the meeting place of the First Continental Congress. A member of the Free Quakers, the fighting Friends who supported the American Revolution, Piles built the Meeting House at Fifth and Arch streets.

The Little House, surveyed by Gunning Bedford and insured by the Philadelphia Contributionship in 1772, as it is today, is a duplicate of the Wister House at 330 South Third. The Little House, however, is arranged in reverse, with the fireplace and staircase to the right of the entrance instead of to the left.

Yellow-pine floor boards on the second and third floors and woodwork at the top of the stairs are original. Three doors, cornice work above the fireplace and one section of the stair rail, all on the second floor, are also those put in by Piles. Eighteenth-century furnishings include a Chippendale secretary and table, English rush-seat chairs, a Queen Anne table and a Hepplewhite candlestand.

Mary, widow of John Piles, sold the house to Bernard Ferris, flour merchant, in 1804. Ferris' widow sold it to John Mohr in 1861, and it remained in the Mohr family until 1907. After that there was a series of owners until 1957, when the house was restored by Robert Trump and purchased by Mr. and Mrs. Lewis M. Robbins, of Haddonfield, New Jersey, who use it as a town house.

The Little House is open to the public only for house tours.

The Little House

THE MAN FULL OF TROUBLE INN and THE PASCHALL HOUSE

To the left is the Paschall house and to the right the famous Man Full of Trouble Inn, 127 Spruce Street.

Man Full of Trouble Inn, showing second-story porch and sign.

THE MAN FULL OF
TROUBLE INN and
THE PASCHALL HOUSE

Man Full of Trouble sign.

James F. Watson, in his famous but not always accurate "Annals," written in 1842, says:

"On the north side of Spruce Street, east of Second Street is a small alley which runs into Dock Street. In this alley more than fifty years ago was an ancient tavern with a very attractive sign, having on it a man and his wife, the latter leaning on his arm. In the hand of the woman was a bandbox and a cat on top of it. The man had a monkey on his shoulder and a parrot in his hand. It was intended to represent 'A Man Full of Trouble.' This tavern retained this name for more than a hundred years."

The tavern is said to be the oldest building in Philadelphia used for that purpose. The inn is believed to have been built in 1759 or 1760 and kept as a tavern by respectable widows or retired sailors. Visitors today may see ships moving up and down the Delaware, and when the old warehouses that deny the inn a full view of the river are torn down it will be easy to imagine the old-time sailors leaving their ships for refreshment at the Man Full of Trouble, just up the hill from the waterfront.

In 1829 it was acquired by Nicholas Stafford and became known as Stafford's Inn. When purchased and restored, with the Paschall House, 127 Spruce Street, by the Wilhelm F. Knauer Foundation in 1965, it was being used as a produce market. The Paschall House, to the west, was built in 1760 by Benjamin Paschall on part of a 1684 proprietary grant. The house has had a succession of owners throughout the years, most of them renting it to others who operated small businesses.

The building is of red brick, two and a half stories high, with a bar and dining room together on the main floor and two bedrooms on each of the upper floors. Off one bedroom is a small porch overlooking the river. The inn has a pent eave and half-gambrel roof. Outside stands a reproduction of the old Man Full of Trouble sign.

Mr. and Mrs. Knauer have repainted the rooms in their original colors. The fireplaces and the paneling on the second floor are original, once stolen from the building but later recovered. The woodwork on the first floor is a reproduction. The fireplace facings are Bristol Delft tiles, copies of some found in a trash heap in the rear of the inn.

81

Man Full of Trouble Inn. Left, east bedroom, showing original paneling, an old cradle, Windsor chair and handsome chest-on-frame. Below, left, another view of bedroom, showing old four-poster bed, crewelwork curtains and antique pewter chamberpot. Below, right, smaller second-floor bedroom, showing original paneling and copies of original Delft tiles facing fireplace.

Dining room of Man Full of Trouble Inn, with antique dresser and collection of Lambeth blue-dash chargers, Bristol Delft and other rare china.

The Knauers have furnished the inn with a collection of fine old antiques. The bar, similar to one in Williamsburg, is lined with old pewter mugs, and there is an old dresser filled with original china, including Lambeth blue-dash Delft chargers, Bristol Delft posset pots and Liverpool puzzle jugs. There is an antique pewter chamber pot in one bedroom.

Among the antique furniture there are a Philadelphia chest-on-frame, tea tables, bow-back Windsor chairs that once belonged to John Jay, a pewter cupboard and original crewelwork curtains. The basement kitchen contains antique fireplace equipment, and there is a partially excavated tunnel, now bricked in, which led toward Dock Creek, a stream, currently covered over, that ran into the Delaware.

The Inn and Paschall House are open as a museum from 1:30 to 4:30 p.m., Tuesday through Sunday. Hostesses, in Colonial costumes, are members of the Colonial Philadelphia Historical Society.

OVERLEAF: Bar and dining room of Man Full of Trouble Inn. The bar is similar to the one in the Raleigh Tavern, Williamsburg.

83

Original fireplace in basement of Man Full of Trouble Inn, now equipped with antique cooking implements, including spit and kettle on a crane.

The Man Full of Trouble Inn and The Paschall House

The Meredith House   The Meredith house, 700 South Washington Square, is an outstanding example of Federal architecture with Georgian characteristics.

Detail of doorway in front parlor of Meredith house, showing elaborate carving. The doors are mahogany. FACING PAGE: View from hall looking into vestibule of the Meredith house.

THE MEREDITH HOUSE

The Meredith House, 700 South Washington Square, built between 1818 and 1823 for merchant Asaph Stone, is an outstanding example of Federal architecture with Georgian characteristics. Three and a half stories, with a dormer window in the half story, it is red brick with white trim. It has graceful, curving white marble steps and a delicate wrought-iron railing leading from the street to the white front door, above which is a fanlight typical of Philadelphia houses built in the 1820-1850 period. The windows have white marble keystones with splayed brick arches. Handsome ironwork graces the second-story back porch and the areaway that leads to the English basement on Seventh Street.

At the house entrance is a vestibule with a carved ceiling and a second door, also with a fanlight. A handsome double parlor, to the left of the hall, is separated by mahogany doors with delicately carved trim at the top of the door frame. The front hall has a carved arch leading to a graceful circular staircase that ascends three flights to a glass dome. The carved, column-decorated marble mantelpieces are similar to those in Mrs. Joseph Carson's house nearby, differing only in being of almost-black Scotch marble instead of being dark gray.

Philadelphia Historical Commission records state that James Meredith bought the house in 1835. It was purchased by Charles Penrose in 1850 for Miss Valeria F. Penrose, who died in 1881. The house was then occupied by Miss Lydia Penrose until her death in 1927.

Apparently none of the distinguished Penroses ever lived here. Dr. Charles Penrose and U. S. Senator Boies Penrose were both born at 1331 Spruce Street, home of their father, attorney Charles Penrose. Boies Penrose 2d, of Devon, Pennsylvania, writes, "I remember going to the Washington Square house as a boy to see my great aunt Lydia, but she was very old and didn't 'track' very well. I don't recall much about the house except that it was frumpy and overfurnished."

Mr. and Mrs. Lawrence M. C. Smith, of Germantown, Pennsylvania, bought the house in 1961. Mr. Smith is a descendant of William Meredith, a prominent lawyer in the early nineteenth century, who was a resident of the

The Meredith House

Curved, carved ceiling in vestibule of Meredith house.
FACING PAGE: Carved arch leading to graceful staircase in Meredith house.

house when he died in 1844.

One of the few old residences left standing on Washington Square, a reminder of the elegance of early nineteenth-century houses, the Meredith House is now given over to offices and apartments. It is impracticable to photograph much of the interior, as fireplaces are obscured by office furniture and apartments occupy the second and third floors. Some idea of its former condition may be gained through an early Contributionship survey of 702 South Washington Square, a similar house once occupied by Peter McCall, mayor of Philadelphia:

. . . the first floor consists of two rooms and a passage with plaster architraves, rounded door and windows, marble mantels with plain columns, mahogany doors with silver-plated hinges and knobs, an arch in the passage with open pilasters, a Venetian door (?) with circular sash, outside shutters, front and back, the second story similar, third story three rooms, and garret three rooms. The stairs are open with a newell, plain brackets and turned banisters, mahogany rail, basement kitchen.

The Meredith House

Taken from the stairwell looking up, this photograph shows the dome on top of the Meredith house.

Iron fence around the areaway leading to the basement kitchen at the Meredith house. Heavier in design than the iron railing leading to the front door, it may have been made at a later date.

Three eighteenth-century row houses just off Washington Square on Seventh Street, as seen from the south. They are adjacent to the Meredith house, 700 South Washington Square.

FACING PAGE: The Morris house, 225 South Eighth Street, built in 1787, is one of the most important in Society Hill.

The Meredith House

THE MORRIS HOUSE

The front door of the Morris house is typical of the 1780-1820 period except that it opens down the middle vertically. Note the old footscraper on the left.

The Morris House

THE MORRIS HOUSE

The Morris House, 225 South Eighth Street, is historically one of the most important houses in Society Hill. Built in 1787, it is entirely original except for an addition in the rear. It has been called "by far the handsomest old city residence of brick that remains in anything like its original condition" in Philadelphia, and the elegance and character of its façade pronounced "unexcelled in early American architecture."

The house, built by "William Reynolds, Doctor of Physick, and his brother John, gentleman brickmaker," is L-shaped, three and a half stories high. It has a solid foundation and is made of Flemish bond — headers and stretchers alternating. The headers are glazed. The front windows have white-marble lintels, with radiating stones centering in keystones above each one. The door, typical of the period 1780-1820, has a pediment, fanlight and keystone with reeded pilasters. To the left of the entrance is an iron foot-scraper, worn thin by generations of use. The façade bears the firemarks of both the Hand-in-Hand and the Green Tree. Under the eaves on the right is a white marble stone marked *1787*.

Inside there is a narrow entrance hall that runs through the house to the garden in the rear. A stairway, in the mode of the period, goes straight up to a landing and, there turning, continues to the second floor.

To the right is the large south parlor, filled with heirlooms of the Morris family, who acquired the house in 1817, and other pieces collected by Harry A. Batten, chairman of the executive committee of N. W. Ayer & Son, present owners who restored the mansion in 1957. Several of the pieces are excellent examples of Philadelphia Chippendale, including two mahogany chairs with cabriole legs, claw-and-ball feet and shell designs, and a slant-top desk with claw-and-ball feet. The fireplaces in the north and south parlors are similar, with built-out chimney breasts and delicate carving on mantelpieces and panels above.

The smaller north parlor, to the left of the entrance, has a Sheraton secretary bookcase. What appear to be two upper drawers let down to make a desk. Behind the dining room, which contains a Hepplewhite serpentine-front sideboard, is a charming old kitchen with the original open fireplace for cooking.

During the latter part of the nineteenth century the south parlor or drawing room was deepened by the addition of a bay, and a pantry and kitchen were built at the end of the rear wing. Bedrooms were also added on the second and third floors above the wing.

On the original second and third floors there are several handsome bedrooms with fireplaces and antique pieces, including chests and four-poster beds as well as a number of mirrors from colonial days. Several rear bedrooms have been furnished in Pennsylvania Dutch style.

When the Reynolds brothers built the house in 1787 its location was considered 'way out in the country. East across the meadows was Potter's Field — later Washington Square — where many Revolutionary soldiers lie buried. Beyond, at Sixth and Walnut streets, was New Prison; to the north, the State House. All the rest, except for the Pennsylvania Hospital, at Eighth and Spruce, was field and orchard.

In 1796, John Reynolds, having speculated in real estate, had overreached himself. As a result the fine house was sold at a sheriff's sale to Ann Dunkin, shopkeeper and widow of a merchant, for $5950. Luke Wistar Morris bought the place in 1817, and subsequently it was occupied by seven generations of the Morris family, until its 1957 purchase by N. W. Ayer. The original Morris, Anthony, came to Philadelphia in 1685 and later served as mayor of the city. A descendant, Samuel Morris, was Captain of the Philadelphia Troop of Light Horse in the Revolution. Luke Wistar Morris was his son.

In restoring the house, the craftsmen removed layers of wallpaper and painted the walls white and the woodwork gray or ashes-of-roses. The walls were originally tinted, it is believed, in pastel shades of whitewash, with the woodwork a mustard color.

One of the most interesting pieces in the Morris house is a clock, made in 1730 by William Ericke, London, fretted in gold and bronze in the Chinese style. There are sixteen bullet holes in its pendulum case, it having become, according to early owner James Alan, "a target to rude and barbarous soldiery" during the Revolution. In the pendulum case may be discerned the words, written in Colonial style:

I brave the times that try'd men's souls
During OUR REVOLUTION:
And have survived the BULLET HOLES,
That won US Constitution.

OLD TIME foresaw the event and cry'd,
Abhor a dissolution;
Endure the Shock with manly Pride,
And boast a Constitution.

Used today as a guest house by N. W. Ayer, the Morris House is open to visitors only on certain house tours.

The Morris House

The Morris house as seen from the garden. This shows the less elaborate window trim in the rear, a door with a fanlight and a large window in the south parlor that was added at a later date. A wistaria vine grows over the trellis and the lawn is edged with boxwood and daffodils in season.

Mantelpiece in the south parlor of the Morris house is faced with marble.

The Morris House

Doorway of Morris house from within, showing graceful carving and box lock. To the left is the famous clock, dated 1730 and, according to an early owner, "a target to rude and barbarous soldiery" during the Revolution.

101

Above the mantelpiece in the Morris house dining room is a blown-up photograph of a print showing the Philadelphia harbor in Revolutionary times. The chandelier is Waterford and the sideboard is Hepplewhite.

The Morris House

The old Morris house kitchen, where meals were prepared in the fireplace in the eighteenth century.

The Pennsylvania Dutch rooms of the Morris house were added in the nineteenth century. Note the unusual hardware on the two closet doors in one of the bedrooms.

The Morris House

MUTUAL ASSURANCE COMPANY

Offices of the Mutual Assurance Company, at Fourth and Locust streets, occupy the Cadwalader house, on the left, and the Shippen-Wistar house, on the right. They are two of the finest old houses preserved in Society Hill.

A close-up of the Cadwalader house, 240 South Fourth Street, occupied by the Mutual Assurance Company.

MUTUAL ASSURANCE COMPANY

This picture shows the second-floor staircase in the Cadwalader house, 240 South Fourth Street, occupied by the Mutual Assurance Company.

When the Philadelphia Contributionship ceased to insure houses surrounded by trees (the directors having decided trees were a fire hazard), the Mutual Assurance Company, Fourth and Locust streets, was founded in 1784. Among the sixty-one founders were Dr. Benjamin Rush, Jared Ingersoll, Samuel Powel and Thomas Willing. For a firemark, the Mutual selected a tree shaped of lead, and from this badge Philadelphia's second mutual fire-insurance Company came to be known as the "Green Tree."

The Green Tree now has its offices in two of the finest early American houses in Society Hill — the Cadwalader House, 240 South Fourth Street, and the Shippen-Wistar House next door, which fronts on Locust Street.

Nathaniel Burt, in *The Perennial Philadelphians,* calls the Cadwalader house "a flawless specimen of early nineteenth-century neo-classic elegance, modest but still noble." The exterior, of red brick with white trim, has a plain cornice, two dormer windows in the garret and doors with fanlights typical of the 1820-1850 period.

The second-floor front and back parlors are in the original Empire style, with gilt decora-

tions on doors and door frames and above the windows. The trustees meet in the front parlor for their monthly dinner (luncheon, in the summer). Dinner is served on china decorated with a green tree, amid a profusion of silver tankards and candelabra. A copper plate on the back of each chair bears the name of a trustee. Among the pieces in the dining room are a Hepplewhite sideboard and a portrait of S. Weir Mitchell done by John Singer Sargent. The curtains, of gold and rose damask by Scalamandre Silks, Inc., were especially woven from a design in the Philippe de LaSalle Museum in France.

The back parlor, where guests gather before dinner, has similar curtains and chair covers; in it are a Rembrandt Peale portrait of Washington and a rare Duplessis portrait of Franklin, done when the great man was our ambassador to France. Also in the building are a Thomas Eakins portrait of General Cadwalader and an unusual Empire chair similar to those chosen by Mrs. John F. Kennedy when she refurnished part of the White House.

The Cadwalader house was built about 1828 by Joseph Parker Norris, Jr., but because of financial reverses he never lived in it. It was

Front parlor of the Cadwalader house, where the trustees of the Mutual Assurance Company hold their dinner meetings.

purchased in 1837 by John Cadwalader, who became Judge of the United States District Court and was for many years solicitor for the Green Tree. His brother, General George Cadwalader, who served in the Mexican War, was chairman of the board of Green Tree.

When Judge Cadwalader's widow died in 1889, the house passed to Dr. Charles E. Cadwalader, a charming and generous bachelor. Seeking refuge from various claimant fiancées, according to Nicholas B. Wainwright, Dr. Cadwalader married his young housekeeper, Mary Ryan, in 1897, setting off waves of publicity across the country. In 1904, the doctor moved to England with his bride, selling the house's contents, except for the silver, which he took along, and the family portrait, which went to the Historical Society of Pennsylvania. The furniture was sold at auction, part of it ending up in the Metropolitan Museum.

Above, right, the Rembrandt Peale portrait of Washington in the back parlor of the Cadwalader house. Below, the famous Duplessis portrait of Franklin, also in the back parlor of the Cadwalader house.

The Shippen-Wistar house, of simpler design than the Cadwalader house, has three stories and an attic. It is built of Flemish bond bricks, with brick belt courses between the floors. The front entrance has marble steps, wrought-iron railings and a fanlight above the door.

By Letters Patent, Proprietors Thomas and Richard Penn granted a plot of land between Walnut and Spruce streets to Joseph and William Shippen in 1744. The grant included the land on the southwest corner of Fourth Street and Prune (now Locust) Street.

In a partition, this corner lot was awarded to William Shippen and it remained in his family until 1797. It was acquired in 1798 by Dr. Caspar Wistar, who built a house there and lived in it until his death in 1818. A distinguished physician, Dr. Wistar was greatly interested in all scientific work; he was an early member of the American Philosophical

This attractive staircase in the Shippen-Wistar house, now occupied by the Mutual Assurance Company, is entirely original.

Taken from the second-floor window of the Shippen-Wistar house, this picture shows the charming garden in the rear.

Society and became its president. Michaux, the botanist and his friend and admirer, named the wistaria vine after him.

It was in this house, on Sunday evenings, that members of the Philosophical Society met as guests of Dr. Wistar. When he died, his friends continued these regular gatherings, calling them "Wistar Parties." With the customary time changed to Saturday evening, these Wistar Parties go on to this day, being held in members' homes or, as they have grown in size, in clubs and other institutions.

The Green Tree has two beautiful gardens on Locust Street, one on the grounds of the insurance company and the other across the street. In 1965 the Pennsylvania Horticultural Society awarded these gardens a gold-medal certificate for their attractive design and well kept appearance. James E. Gowen is the board chairman today.

The Mutual Assurance Company

Front-parlor mantelpiece in the Shippen-Wistar house has delicate carving and fluting and Pennsylvania blue-marble facings. The rare eighteenth-century American clock is of mahogany, with satinwood marqueterie fans and borders, a silvered dial displaying numerals and an eagle and the name *Makeway*.

Old Pine Street Presbyterian Church, on the south side of Pine between Fourth and Fifth streets, constructed in 1768, was altered extensively in the nineteenth century.

OLD PINE STREET CHURCH

Chartered as the Third Presbyterian Church in Philadelphia, the Old Pine Street Church is the only Presbyterian edifice preserved from the colonial period, and one of eight colonial churches still standing in the city. It was founded in 1768 by members of the First Presbyterian Church and others who were worshiping in the small Hill Meeting House on the site of the present building at Fourth and Pine streets. The land had been granted to the congregation "for the use of Presbyterians forever" by Letters Patent signed by Thomas and Richard Penn in 1764. It was here that George Whitefield, after being refused the use of other churches, preached from a stage erected by his friends.

The present building, constructed in 1768 in eighteenth-century style, was altered in 1837, in 1857 and again in 1867, the roof and floor being raised and the entrance portico and columns added. It is a handsome example of Greek Revival, popular about 1830. The front has eight Corinthian fluted columns in white marble, a portico and a pediment. Inside there are two fluted columns and two pilasters before the sanctuary and elaborate carving along the walls of the gallery. The pews appear to be twentieth-century.

The Old Pine Street Church

Organ and gallery in Old Pine Street Church.

The first pastor of "Old Pine" was the Reverend George Duffield, who was also Chaplain of the Continental Congress and of the Pennsylvania Militia in the Revolution. The British set a price on Dr. Duffield's head. He is buried under the sanctuary, beneath the gravestone in the floor of the lower room, one of the few intramural graves found in Presbyterian churches.

Two signers of the Declaration of Independence, John Adams and Dr. Benjamin Rush, attended Old Pine. Another medical man who attended services here in Revolutionary days was Dr. William Shippen, Jr., first professor of medicine in America and Director-General of hospitals during the War for Independence.

Sixty-seven men from Old Pine went into the Revolutionary army, thirty-five of them as commissioned officers. One of them was General John Steele, Washington's personal aide-de-camp in New Jersey, who also served as a field officer at Yorktown on the day of Cornwallis' surrender. General Steele is buried in the churchyard. So are William Hurrie, bell ringer of the State House (now Independence Hall), who is believed to have rung the Liberty Bell at the first public reading of the Declaration; Jared Ingersoll, a signer of the Constitution; Colonel William Linnard, Revolutionary soldier and Quartermaster-General in the War of 1812; and Mrs. Mary Nelson, who was a childhood playmate of George IV and had

Interior of Old Pine Street Church, showing gallery and carved columns framing sanctuary.

charge of the Philadelphia powder magazine in the War of 1812.

While occupying Philadelphia during the Revolution, the British used Old Pine as a hospital and burned the pews for fuel. A hundred Hessian soldiers are buried in the yard.

After World War II the Friends of Old Pine raised funds for a major restoration of the church building. In 1953 the congregation of Old Pine merged with that of Hollond-Scots Church, adopting the name Third and Scots Presbyterian Church. About half of the $240,-000 needed for the restoration was contributed through the Friends of Old Pine and the rest came from the sale of the Hollond-Scots property.

In 1957 the Philadelphia Planning Commission and the Redevelopment Authority recommended that the whole block between Fourth and Fifth streets and Pine and Lombard streets be reserved for church use. They suggested that a building be provided to house the records of the United Presbyterian Church, now in the headquarters of the Presbyterian Historical Society, located in the Witherspoon Building. It is hoped that adequate quarters near Old Pine will be built for this purpose.

The church, which will celebrate its bicentennial in 1968, has had many distinguished pastors. The Reverend John H. Leitch is in charge of Old Pine today.

The church is open to the public daily from nine to five.

OVERLEAF: Elaborate columns, with carved entablature above, were added to frame the Old Pine Street Church sanctuary.

Statue of William Penn stands before main building of Pennsylvania Hospital. Note the white marble facing to the second floor, pilasters with Corinthian capitals, cornice and pediment with modillions.

THE PENNSYLVANIA HOSPITAL

The Pennsylvania Hospital, on Pine Street between Eighth and Ninth, was built in 1755, the first hospital in the colonies. It was designed by Samuel Rhoads, one of the institution's managers. Benjamin Franklin was elected president.

The hospital is built of red brick, with white-marble and wooden trim. The east wing, which is the oldest part, is set in Flemish bond. The original front door, in the center building on Pine Street, has been termed "the finest example of Adamesque architecture in colonial America." The door has an elaborate fanlight above and columns on either side.

The center house, built between 1794 and 1805 — David Evans, Jr., architect — shows a sophisticated bay of four marble pilasters contrasting with red brickwork. A central dome was planned but never built; a surgical amphitheater with skylight took its place. The beautiful iron gates on Pine Street were closed in 1824, following Lafayette's visit to Dr. Philip Syng Physick, and were not opened again until May 3, 1965, when the hospital marked the bicentennial of the University of Pennsylvania Medical School.

The Pennsylvania Hospital

The original door of the main building, Pennsylvania Hospital, has been called "the finest example of Adamesque architecture in Colonial America." FACING PAGE: Following Lafayette's visit to Dr. Philip Syng Physick in 1824, this east gate of Pennsylvania Hospital was closed, not to be opened again until May 3, 1965.

The hospital was founded by Dr. Thomas Bond. Among those who have served in it are many others famous in the medical annals of Philadelphia and the nation. They include Dr. Philip Syng Physick, originator of the stomach pump; Dr. William Shippen, Jr., who first introduced medical teaching in this country; Dr. Caspar Wistar, anatomy teacher credited with the first anatomical textbook here; Dr. John Morgan, who founded the University of Pennsylvania Medical School; Dr. Benjamin Rush, "Father of Psychological Medicine"; and Dr. Thomas Story Kirkbride, pioneer in the care of the mentally ill.

The Pennsylvania Hospital has cared for the sick and wounded in wartime as well as in peace, its activity unabated during the Revo-

lution, the War of 1812, the Civil War, the Spanish-American War and the two World Wars. During World War I, Pennsylvania Base Hospital Unit No. 10 went to France and in World War II the institution sponsored a group called Evacuation Hospital No. 52.

Over the years numerous additions have been made to the hospital. They include the women's building, the Benjamin Franklin Clinic and the nurses' residence. The 162-bed J. Henry Scheidt Building, completed in 1963, was the first step in a $19,000,000 improvement plan.

The hospital has a painting by Benjamin West, "Christ Healing the Sick in the Temple," donated by him in 1817. Another interesting item is a plaque set above the corner-

SOUTH EAST VIEW OF THE PENNSYLVANIA HOSPITAL

This old print of Pennsylvania Hospital shows how the buildings appeared in the early nineteenth century. *Photo by Robert Halvey, courtesy Pennsylvania Hospital.*

stone bearing an inscription by Benjamin Franklin and installed with Masonic rites on May 28, 1755; it reads:

In the year of Christ
MDCCLV
George the Second happily reigning
(For he sought the happiness of his people)
Philadelphia flourishing
(For its inhabitants were publick spirited)
This building
By the bounty of the government
And of many private persons
was piously founded
For the relief of the sick and miserable
May the God of mercies
Bless the undertaking.

An annual Pennsylvania Day fete and house tour, inaugurated by the women's auxiliary in 1948, is held each June, on either the first or second Wednesday. The fair, which includes an exhibition of obedience by dogs and a fashion show presented by Gimbels, was originally held on the hospital lawn facing Pine Street but the event soon grew so big that it was moved to Washington Square. Mrs. Peyton R. Biddle, chairman of the women's auxiliary, says that more than 5000 attend the fair each year. In 1965 a tour of Society Hill was included; in 1966 the auxiliary may sponsor a bus tour of historic spots or another house tour.

Benjamin West's famous painting, "Christ Healing the Sick in the Temple," hangs in the Eighth Street-entrance lobby of the Pennsylvania Hospital.

THE PHILADELPHIA CONTRIBUTIONSHIP

Founded by Benjamin Franklin in 1752, the Philadelphia Contributionship for the Insurance of Houses from Loss by Fire, 212 South Fourth Street, is the oldest insurance company in the United States. It is familiarly known as the Contributionship, or the "Hand-in-Hand" (the company's firemark is four clasped hands).

The Contributionship's first office was in the home of Joseph Saunders, a Quaker merchant who agreed to serve as its first clerk for an annual salary of forty pounds. Saunders lived, according to Nicholas B. Wainwright, "a few yards from the Delaware River."

The company was next housed in the residence of Caleb Carmalton, between Second and Third at 99 High Street, now 239 Market Street. Starting as a clerk in 1776, Mr. Carmalton served with the Contributionship during the Revolution and later, covering the time when the Constitutional Convention was in session and the decade when Philadelphia was the national capital. Presidents George Washington and John Adams lived only a few blocks west of him. He retired in 1817, shortly before his death.

The company next had an office at 109 Dock Street, and moved into its present quarters on Fourth Street, near Walnut, in 1836. Thomas U. Walter was engaged to design and erect a suitable building for a dwelling and office. One of the leaders in the Greek Revival movement, Walter had designed Girard College, "Andalusia," the Biddle mansion on the Delaware, and had supervised plans for the expansion of the Capitol in Washington. The handsome brick building he completed for the Contributionship was designed to provide office space and a directors' room as well as to accommodate the treasurer and his family. (In those days the treasurer lived above the office in order to guard the company's assets.)

The building has four Corinthian columns, two fluted pilasters and a balustrade, all of white marble, on either side of the entrance. The façade is in the Empire style, with double windows separated by pilasters and a dentil cornice.

The business offices are on the first floor. On the second floor are three handsome meeting rooms; to the north, the full length of the

FACING PAGE: This 1836 Greek Revival building, at 212 South Fourth Street, is now occupied by the Philadelphia Contributionship for Insuring Houses from Loss By Fire, the oldest mutual fire-insurance company in the United States.

125

On one of the matching mantelpieces in the gold room of the Philadelphia Contribution-ship are a pair of French urns with portraits of Napoleon and Josephine and a crystal candelabrum, English Bristol c. 1810. The portrait reflected in the mirror is one of the late J. Rodman Paul, a director from 1895 to 1925.

Board room on the second floor of the Philadelphia Contributionship building, where the directors' meetings are held, with an Empire mahogany extension table, curly-maple side chairs and a black-marble mantelpiece matching one in the dining room.

building, is the gold room, where the finance committee meets, around an eighteenth-century English Sheraton table. There are two marble fireplaces with mirrors above them. To the south — toward the street — is the board room. Facing the garden is a dining room, where, on the third Wednesday of each month, as they have done since the company was founded, the directors dine. The third floor, once occupied by the treasurer and his family, now contains employees' rest rooms.

The furniture is mainly Empire, with tremendous mahogany tables and sideboards, crystal chandeliers and curly-maple chairs, *circa* 1836. Some of the chairs bear hooks on which to hang fire screens for protecting the directors from the heat of the fireplace. Decorating the walls are portraits of two centuries of board chairmen, among them many persons famous in Philadelphia annals. H. Gates Lloyd is the current chairman.

Although the pounding of the typewriter has replaced the scratching of quill pens, the company's antique origins remain much in evidence. An old-fashioned desk and inkwells with quill pens may be seen in the rear south office. Also displayed are many old leather fire hats, worn when the firefighting was done by volunteer companies, and an old chest in which the company's valuables are said to have been hidden and buried during the Revolution. (The chest was ordered to be made at a board meeting in 1776, "wherein to deposit the Books, Papers, Deeds of Settlement, etc. belonging to the Contributionship that the same may be removed to a place of safety in case of danger.")

There is a most attractive garden with a fountain in the rear of the building. Before the Revolution, the directors of the Contributionship, using funds that had accumulated from fines levied for tardiness or absence at board meetings, placed milestones along the King's Highway to the south. The nineteenth milestone now stands in the rear of the garden.

Visitors to the Contributionship are welcome.

Directors' dining room of the Philadelphia Contributionship, with Empire mahogany dining table, serving table, sideboard and curly-maple armchairs and Sheffield candelabra. Mahogany tall case clock made by Abel Panchaud, Oxford Street. The crystal chandelier came from an old house at 1008 Spruce Street. The black-marble mantelpiece bears a woodcock under glass.

Gold room of the Contributionship, showing the eighteenth-century English Sheraton mahogany table. Twenty-seven feet long and with five pedestals, it is displayed in two sections. The chairs are reproductions.

Old desk where clerks wrote with quill pens, at the Philadelphia Contributionship. Above is a picture of founder Benjamin Franklin and a row of leather fire hats dated 1752 and 1760. Below are fire buckets, also leather, dated 1787, on a chest in which the fire-insurance company's valuable papers were hidden during the Revolution.

Garden in rear of Philadelphia Contributionship contains a fountain (covered over in photo), paths lined with boxwood and a rare magnolia, *kobus borealis*.

Close-up of Portico Row house, showing Ionic-columned porticos, wrought-iron railings and areaways with steps to what originally were basement kitchens.

The houses on Portico Row, south side of Spruce Street between Ninth and Tenth, were built in 1831-32 in Greek Revival style.

Portico Row, the block between Ninth and Tenth streets on the south side of Spruce, is actually one block outside the limits of Society Hill, but its houses are so charming and different — each having a white-marble portico with Ionic capitals on the columns — that they deserve presentation here. They are three-story brick houses, built in 1831 and 1832.

An insurance survey made of the house at 902 Spruce in 1839 states: "... the floors are wide yellow pine, there are pilasters, full cornices, Italian marble hearths and mahogany doors. There are two arches in the vestibule and two Grecian marble mantels with full columns. The staircase has two turned birdseye ballusters [sic] and a mahogany rail." Unfortunately, no pictures of the interiors could be made for this volume.

When these houses were first built they were owned or occupied by members of many prominent old Philadelphia families, and well known names have continued to be connected with them. Some of them have been: William Penn Gaskell Hall, Warner Fairfax Washington, Robert Toland, Colonel William Drayton, Mrs. J. Madison Taylor, Mr. and Mrs. Charles Stewart Wurts (who lived at 926 from 1911 to 1956) and Mr. and Mrs. Charles Wharton.

The one at 700 Spruce belongs to the Pennsylvania Hospital and the others are now rooming houses, the property of various owners. The Redevelopment Authority hopes that eventually they will be restored as apartments if not as regular dwellings. They are of course large, and most people moving into the Society Hill area prefer small houses.

Portico Row

THE POWEL HOUSE

This original staircase in the Powel house is paneled with solid Santo Domingo mahogany. Twist on staircase rail is a restoration.

The Powel House, 244 South Third Street, has been called the handsomest Georgian house in Society Hill. Built in 1765 by Charles Stedman, it was purchased in 1768 by Samuel Powel, who served as mayor of Philadelphia under the British Crown, 1775-1776, and was also the city's first mayor under the new republic, 1789-1790.

When, due to financial reverses, Stedman had been forced to sell the house, he advertised in the *Pennsylvania Gazette* as follows:

To be sold by Charles Stedman, a large well finished commodious house three stories high 31 feet front and 46 feet deep with large convenient back buildings, 76 feet deep and two stories high situated on the west side of Third Street on a lot clear of ground rent adjoining the house the Governor lives in, with the privilege of an alley 3 feet, 6 inches wide; the lot runs into Fourth Street, 396 feet deep, on which stands a new brick stable, two stories high, 26 feet by 20.

Powel paid £3150 for the house, which later numbered Washington and Lafayette among its distinguished visitors. During the Revolution, the Earl of Carlisle lived in it, with Mr. and Mrs. Powel moving to the back buildings.

The house is built of bricks, set in Flemish bond — headers and stretchers alternating. Over each window is a keystone of white marble, with matching belt courses of marble between first and second and second and third floors. The shutters have four panels; the window panes are six above and six below; there is a splayed brick arch above each window.

The front door has eight panels and there is a fanlight above the door frame, which is supported by two Doric columns, with a pilaster behind each column. The entablature above the door is in three parts, with architrave, frieze and cornice with dentils. Because of the colonial box lock used the door knob is set four inches from the edge of the door. The original front door lock was restored by the Descendants of the Signers of the Declaration of Independence.

The archway in the front hall, also original, returned to the house by the Philadelphia

FACING PAGE: Powel house, 244 South Third Street, showing the dormers.
Picture from Interiors *magazine, courtesy Malcolm Smith, Inc.*

135

Interior view of the front door of the Powel house, showing fanlight and eight-paneled door. The box lock is a restoration.

Museum of Art, was restored in 1931 by the city's Society for the Preservation of Landmarks. There is a handsome mahogany staircase with the original treads and spindles; the twist on the stair rail is a restoration. The staircase is paneled with solid Santo Domingo mahogany; the decorative brackets on its outside, originally of handmolded lead, were removed to be made into bullets, it is said — a story that Nicholas Wainright labels "not convincing." They have been replaced by hand-carved wooden replicas.

The most impressive room in the house is the second-floor front drawing room, sometimes described as the ballroom or music room. The two mahogany doors flanking the fireplace are original; the rest of the room is a restoration — the work of the Landmarks Society. The carved tablet above the mantelpiece displays a lamb, a mill and a dog, representing one of Aesop's fables. The carved festoons on either side of the tablet may have been the work of Courtnay. An open pediment above has an armorial cartouche containing a lion. Strings of carven flowers flank the chimney piece and just beneath the pediment frame is a swelled carved frieze broken by a plain tablet.

The mahogany doors are set in ornately carved frames and finished with open pediments. Carved baseboard, chair rails and panel moldings add further decoration. The ceiling is ornamented with ribbons, flowers, fruit and musical instruments, rendered in plaster.

The second-floor back parlor, the original of which is now in the Metropolitan Museum, has a door leading to the drawing room. Here too there are handsome carvings above the mantelpiece and plaster molding on the ceiling, although not as elaborate as that in the drawing room. The Landmarks Society has furnished it as a bedroom.

Downstairs are a reception room and a dining room. The back buildings contain offices, kitchen and additional bedrooms.

The house is furnished mainly with Philadelphia antiques, many of them in it when it was occupied by the Powels. Among the items are a Joseph Richardson, Jr., silver coffeepot, Nanking china and a Martha Washington sewing table given to Mrs. Powel by Mrs. Washington. A fire screen in the first-floor reception room is a Powel family piece; so is a wooden sun dial, on a wall of the porch between the front and back buildings, that is marked *S.P.* and inscribed *I count Life by sunny hours and them alone.*

The mansion is open daily, except Sunday, from ten to five.

136

This handsomely carved mantelpiece and overmantel with broken pediment from the Powel house is now in the Philadelphia Museum of Art. *Courtesy Philadelphia Museum of Art.*

This photo shows the treatment of all interior doors in the Powel house, except those in the drawing room: an open pediment with dentils.

The Powel House

OVERLEAF: Powel house drawing room. The entire interior of this room was removed to the Philadelphia Museum of Art and furnished with eighteenth-century Philadelphia objects. *Courtesy Philadelphia Museum of Art.*

One of the pair of original mahogany doors that flank the fireplace in the Powel house drawing room, showing the elaborate carving of the door frame, with open pediment supported by trusses and ornately designed frieze, and small flowers or rosettes in the knees or inner corners.

Second-floor rear parlor of the Powel house, removed to the Metropolitan Museum of Art. The wallpaper was added by the museum. *Courtesy Metropolitan Museum of Art.*

OVERLEAF: Powel house parlor at the Metropolitan Museum of Art, New York, handsomely furnished with an ornate highboy, a plainer lowboy and several eighteenth-century Philadelphia chairs. *Courtesy Metropolitan Museum of Art.*

Powel house parlor, now in the Metropolitan Museum of Art, showing the carved marble-faced mantelpiece and overmantel with broken pediment. *Courtesy Metropolitan Museum of Art.*

Original back buildings of Powel house and part of garden. The buildings contain a porch, offices, kitchens and additional upstairs bedrooms. The antique English sun dial is a gift of the Soroptimist Club of Philadelphia.

The Powel House

ST. JOSEPH'S, WILLING'S ALLEY

Entrance from Willing's Alley to Old St. Joseph's Church, showing courtyard beyond. The arch is Greek Revival style.

No book about Society Hill would be complete if it did not include St. Joseph's Church, Willing's Alley. The first public Roman Catholic Church in Philadelphia, it was designated a national shrine by President Dwight D. Eisenhower in 1959.

Father Joseph Greaton, Order of the Society of Jesus, arrived in Philadelphia in 1729. At first he conducted services in private homes for the city's Catholics. In 1733 Father Greaton purchased the land on which St. Joseph's was built, and a year later the new church was completed. St. Joseph's then was the only place in the English-speaking world where public celebration of the Mass was permitted by law, William Penn's Charter of Privileges granting freedom of worship in Pennsylvania.

The original church building, enlarged once in 1757 and again in 1821, was demolished in 1838. The new edifice — today's St. Joseph's — thus is early Victorian. Of red brick with white marble trim, it has a quaint arched entrance into a courtyard from Willing's Alley, between Walnut and Spruce and Third and Fourth streets. Purchase of several properties on Walnut Street by the Department of the Interior has made it possible for the church to be seen from Walnut as well as from Willing's Alley.

The church interior is Colonial in style, painted pale green with some of the woodwork being accented in gold. Behind the altar are four columns and four fluted pilasters, with a semicircular arch resting on the tops of the columns. To the left is a statue of St. Francis Xavier, and to the right one of St. Joseph. They are flanked by altars to the Blessed Mother and the Sacred Heart. A carved marble railing separates the chancel from the body of the church.

A very graceful semicircular gallery is built across the rear of the church. In the gallery there is a handsome organ and organ case, with decorations in relief, painted gold. The pews appear to be of modern oak.

The church, now a part of Independence National Historical Park, is open daily. Father Edmund J. Nuttall, S. J., is pastor.

Organ and gallery, Old St. Joseph's Church.

Altar of Old St. Joseph's Church, with statues of St. Francis Xavier and St. Joseph.

Old St. Paul's Protestant Episcopal Church, built in 1761, was altered in modified Greek Revival style in 1830.

ST. PAUL'S CHURCH

Organized in 1760 at a meeting held in the State House (now Independence Hall), Old St. Paul's Church, 225 South Third Street, was built with funds raised by lottery, considered a perfectly proper method at that time. The building was erected in 1761 and in 1830 it was altered by the famous architect, William Strickland. Like so many other old buildings in Society Hill that have undergone successive changes, which of its parts was built when could be decided only by an architectural detective. It was the third Church of England parish in Philadelphia and very probably looked somewhat like St. Peter's Church inside.

Strickland put high steps in the front and raised the floor so that there would be space for Sunday School classes to meet on the ground level. Of red brick with white trim, the building has four brick pilasters across the front, a white-marble door frame supported by pilasters and arch-topped windows. Brick fence posts bear ornamental white-marble balls. The top of the edifice is finished in a pediment with a round window. The handsome wrought-iron gates were brought from England before the Revolution.

St. Paul's Church

THE LORD IS IN HIS HOLY TEMPLE

Altar in chapel of St. Paul's Church.

Stephen Girard attended St. Paul's and was married to Mary Lum in the church June 6, 1777. Edwin Forrest, the actor who at his death left a fund to establish the Edwin Forrest Home for aged actors, is buried in the church-yard.

In 1901 the Corporation of St. Paul's Church was dissolved and its property turned over to St. Peter's Church. In 1904 St. Peter's gave the land and building to the Episcopal Diocese of Pennsylvania, when it became the headquarters of the Philadelphia Protestant Episcopal City Mission. Today the Episcopal Community Services occupies offices off the main part of the original church and the second-floor galleries.

There is still a chapel with an altar at the east end of the building where services are held. The sanctuary was renovated and the original railing was restored in the chapel in 1957.

The building and chapel are open to the public from 9:00 A.M. to 4:45 P.M., Mondays through Fridays.

Wrought-iron gates at main entrance of St. Paul's Church were brought from England before the Revolution.

St. Peter's Protestant Episcopal Church, Third and Pine streets, showing part of church-yard. Considered one of the finest Georgian churches in the East, it was built in 1761, with tower and steeple added in 1842.

ST. PETER'S CHURCH

Altar and organ

St. Peter's Protestant Episcopal Church, at Third and Pine streets, was built in 1761. One of the finest Early Georgian churches in the United States, it remains today almost exactly as it was more than 200 years ago. Only the stained-glass windows and a church tower and steeple, which replaced the original cupola, have been added. The high-backed box pews, the stone floors, the beautiful wineglass pulpit with its sounding board and its prayer desk underneath and the galleries, running north and south, have remained untouched throughout the years.

The architects were Robert Smith, who also designed Carpenter's Hall, Philadelphia, and Nassau Hall, Princeton, and John Kearsley. The land and churchyard were a grant from Thomas and Richard Penn, proprietors of the colony. A picture, *circa* 1702, shows that the land on which the church was built was then a duck pond, surrounded by Indian tepees. An old lady remembered having picked blackberries there. After the church was built the wife of the rector was given permission to pasture her cow in the churchyard.

The cost of building St. Peters was £4765, 19 shillings, 6½ pence. Funds were raised through contributions from the congregation and later, when there was a deficit, by a lottery. A framed lottery ticket, dated 1765, bearing the inscription *St. Peters & Church Lottery,* may be seen at the church.

According to C. P. Beauchamp Jefferys, whose father, Dr. Edward M. Jefferys, was rector of the church from 1906 to 1937, the decision to build St. Peter's was made when Christ Church, Second and Market streets, was becoming overcrowded and "the long tramp from Society Hill through filthy, muddy streets was becoming more and more distasteful to these fine gentlemen and beautiful belles in damasks and brocades, velvet breeches and silk stockings, powdered hair and periwigs." In March 1753 "some gentlemen from the South End of the city" drew up a petition to present to the Penns. The signers of this petition included many prominent persons of the time, although the only families extant today bearing any of the surnames are Sims and McCall. The Penns made the grant and plans went ahead.

The first service in the new building was held September 4, 1761. Following a procession from Christ Church to St. Peter's, composed of the clergy, vestry, church wardens, clerk, sexton, James Hamilton and members of his Council, and others, Dr. William Smith, Provost of the University of Pennsylvania, preached the sermon. The church has had many distinguished ministers, beginning with Dr. Robert Jenney, who had been rector of Christ Church, and including Bishop William White.

Built of red brick with white trim, the church has an enclosing red brick wall on west, north and east sides. Part of the east wall has been replaced by an iron fence. Quoting C. P. Beauchamp Jefferys:

"The structure is two and a half stories high, having pedimental ends. The round-headed upper windows have fifteen-paned lower sashes and twenty-paned upper, above which twelve keystone-shaped panes and one semicircular pane form the round top. The large chancel window at the east end has 108 rectangular panes in its central section, with twenty-eight keystone-shaped ones arranged around the semicircular one at its round top. On each side of this is a section forming altogether what is called the Palladium. Arranged about this are four smaller round-headed windows, with a circular one in the pediment above.

"Within are the original white square-box pews with doors and seats facing both ways, those of the gallery being similarly arranged. The galleries, supported by plain columns, are paneled in front, as well as the pews, reading desk and pulpit. . . . A feature is the location of the reading desk and pulpit at the west end and the chancel at the east end, compelling the minister to walk down the central aisle from one end to the other, preceded by the verger with his mace. The congregation can face either way.

"Above and behind the pulpit is a molded panel surmounted by a broken pedimental head with a carved floreated design in high relief within the break. Tradition had it that this panel was originally intended to contain the Penn coat of arms but I find no historical evidence of the fact. The structure was surmounted by a small wooden cupola or belfry."

Two old bells from Christ Church were installed in the cupola, and during the Revolution were taken, together with the Liberty Bell and the bells from Christ Church, to Allentown, where they were hidden under the floor of the Zion Reformed Church, to be returned in 1778. Benjamin Chew Wilcocks presented the church with full chimes in 1842, when the present tower and steeple were erected to house them. A ten-foot gilt cross was put atop the steeple, despite the opposition of some members. The first organ, installed in 1764, was placed at the east end in 1789, obscuring some of the east window.

Among the church's treasured possessions are some rare Bibles, one of them a so-called Vinegar Bible. A large Church of England prayer book, inscribed *St. Peter's Church, 1784*, has prayers for "Our most gracious Sovereign Lord King George" and "Our most gracious Queen Charlotte, his royal highness George, Prince of Wales and all the Royal Family" crossed out and a handwritten prayer for the President of the United States substituted. There are portraits by Charles Willson Peale, silver by William Syng and two ornate candlesticks said to have come from the country home of Joseph Bonaparte, near Bordentown, New Jersey.

Buried in the churchyard, besides seven Indian chiefs who died in the smallpox epidemic of 1793, are Benjamin Chew, Chief Justice of the Supreme Court of Pennsylvania; Captain William E. Shippen, killed at the Battle of Princeton, 1777; Nicholas Biddle, president of the Second United States Bank; Charles Willson Peale, artist; George M. Dallas, vice president of the United States; and Stephen Decatur, naval hero. George Washington was a frequent worshiper at St. Peter's, sitting in Pew 41 with his friend Samuel Powel.

St. Peter's had its lean years during the early 1900s, when most of the congregation moved to the country, but with the redevelopment of Society Hill it is beginning its third century with renewed vigor. The Reverend Joseph Koci, Jr., present rector, is raising money to landscape the churchyard, repair the brick wall and iron fence and install posts and lanterns. St. Peter's will be at the head of a new greenway that will bisect the new Society Hill as planned by Philadelphia's Redevelopment Authority.

The church is open to visitors from nine to five daily.

Wineglass pulpit, St. Peter's Church.

THE TRUMP HOUSE

The Trump House, 214 Delancey Street, is the earliest residence, intact with original woodwork — even many window sash — in Society Hill. It still has the original woodwork, paneling, chair rail, old box locks, etc. Built between 1753 and 1756, it was restored by Robert T. Trump, restorationist and antiquarian, in 1955-56. The Powel House, which was restored earlier, is now a public museum.

The Trump House is a charming example of early Philadelphia Colonial, simple in design, of blue glazed brick in Flemish bond pattern, with a pent eave. According to early directories, it was owned and occupied by a retired ship captain from the early 1770s until after the War of 1812, although General Howe's officers reportedly used it during the Revolution.

Mr. and Mrs. Trump have furnished their home with antiques from various periods. Living-room sofa and birdcage table go back to the Federal period of old Philadelphia. The Queen Anne mirror on one wall is from Boston. The andirons are French. Over the fireplace is a self-portrait of Sir Godfrey Kneller, 1646-1723, done *circa* 1700. England's most proficient portrait painter in his time, Sir Godfrey exerted much influence on his country's portraitists through the mid-eighteenth century.

Curtains and slip-covers on the armchairs (non-antique) are blue-and-white linen, a copy of a pattern popular in the time of George II. The glass curtains are of beige Italian silk. Two graceful New York City Federal chairs, painted black with gold trim, have antique gold lampas covers.

The painting hanging above the sofa has an interesting history. It is a picture of Chaulkley Hall, home of Abel James in the Frankford section of Philadelphia, *circa* 1730. James was the staunch anti-tax leader who refused to allow the British tea ship, *Polly*, to land in Philadelphia. The *Polly* later went on to Boston, her arrival there leading to the famous Tea Party. Chaulkley Hall was torn down long before it was thought so important to preserve such relics of the past, but the Metropolitan Museum acquired its front portal and door in 1954. The picture, painted by G. L. Miller in the 1850s, was found by Architect Charles Peterson in a Philadelphia auction-

FACING PAGE: The Trump house, built between 1753 and 1756, is a charming example of early Philadelphia Colonial. Note pent eave, plaster cove cornice, gambrel roof and dormer with flat shed roof.

159

Trump house parlor, showing original paneling.

FACING PAGE: Original paneling in master bedroom of Trump house. Note warming pan and old mirror above mantel.

eer's bargain basement and acquired by Mr. Trump in trade for some antique door hardware.

To the rear of the living room is a room that was the original kitchen, with the old fireplace and crane, now used by the Trumps as a study. A new kitchen has been added, and there is an attractive little city garden.

The master bedroom on the second floor has a fireplace and original paneling. As already noted, considerable of the original woodwork is also found in other parts of the house.

The house is occasionally open to the public for house tours.

Trump house parlor, showing Federal Philadelphia sofa and picture of famous Chaulkley Hall. Original box lock on door.

Trump house garden — brick paved terrace, sun dial and flowers and flowering shrubs in season.

THE WATTS HOUSE

The Henry Miller Watts House, 219 Spruce Street, is not an eighteenth-century house but it was built in eighteenth-century style and it is so elegant in detail that it belongs in this book. Unable to find a Georgian house in Society Hill large and sturdy enough for their needs, Mr. and Mrs. Watts decided to build one. They bought a lot on the north side of Spruce Street, where the Redevelopment Authority had torn down two small houses, and engaged George Brooke Roberts, a leading Philadelphia architect, and Melvin H. Grebe, builder. Mr. Roberts drew plans for a structure that would conform to the eighteenth-century architecture of the neighborhood.

Here, in 1961, was built one of the handsomest houses in Society Hill. Of red brick, with Georgian window frames and shutters, it has a Colonial doorway with two columns and an arch. Firemarks of the Green Tree and the Hand-in-Hand show between the second and third floors.

The visitor enters a black-and-white marble-floored vestibule. A second door leads into a hall with a beautiful elliptical staircase rising two flights to the third floor. There is also an elevator, hidden behind a white paneled door.

Straight ahead, at the far end of the hall, is a small den with a plain fireplace. Mrs. Watts purchased some brown-and-white Delft tiles to liven up the fireplace; much to her delight a workman excavating for the garden later on found a tile identical to the ones she had used. An original St. Memin portrait of an ancestor, St. George Woods, hangs above the fireplace.

To the right is a large dining room with built-in corner cabinets filled with green, white and gold flowered Paris china inherited by Mrs. Watts. The tops of the cabinets are semi-circular, with shell designs; the shelves are shaped. The room has a dentil cornice.

A portrait of Mr. Watts' great-grandfather, the first Henry Miller Watts, hangs above the English antique sideboard. Three rare coconut goblets, made in London in 1782 by T. Daniel for Mrs. Alexander Johnston, Mrs. Watts' great-grandmother, rest on the sideboard. There is also a portrait of General Henry Miller, who fought in the Revolution and for whom the set of Hepplewhite chairs used in the dining room was made.

Dining room and den look out on a handsome Italian garden. Designed by the late Charles Willing, it is ornamented with ever-

The Watts house, 219 Spruce Street.

greens, potted plants, a fountain and two lead urns that originally were in the garden of Harston, Chestnut Hill, formerly the residence of Mrs. Watts' parents, the late Mr. and Mrs. Frazer Harris.

On the second floor is a large living room, built across the entire rear of the house, that opens onto a porch with steps leading down to the garden. Architect Roberts got the idea for this porch from an old house in Alexandria, Virginia. The living room is ornamented with an eighteenth-century carved mantelpiece salvaged from an old house on Philadelphia's Front Street. Its facings are of black and beige Vermont marble. Gesso bas-relief on the panel in the center of the mantel depicts Apollo in a chariot drawn by two lions and attended by various characters of mythology. There are swags on either side, and two Delft-blue tobacco jars rest on the mantelpiece.

Among the family portraits in this room is one of Colonel Francis Johnston, who was a member of Philadelphia's famous First Troop, Philadelphia City Cavalry, and served in the Revolution. The painting is flanked by two mirrored Italian sconces.

The house, elegant and beautifully kept, looks like a museum, but the owners do not treat it as such. They entertain frequently, including very small grandchildren as well as adults.

The Watts House is not open to the public except on house tours.

East end of second-floor living room, Watts house. Portrait above sofa is flanked by antique Italian mirrored sconces.

Watts house den, showing fireplace lined with antique Dutch tiles and St. Memins portrait of a family ancestor.

Eighteenth-century carved mantelpiece above fireplace in Watts house living room came from an old house on Front Street, Philadelphia.

Dining room in Henry Miller Watts house has corner cupboards filled with Paris china. The chairs are Hepplewhite.

The second-floor porch in the rear of the Watts house was modeled after one in Alexandria.

The Watts House

Elliptical staircase in Watts house as seen while looking up from center hall.

OVERLEAF: Elliptical staircase in Watts house, looking down two flights to marble tiled floor of hall.

The Wister house, left, and the Little house were built as a pair about 1771.

THE WISTER HOUSE

The William Wister House, 330 South Third Street, was known in Colonial days as a faith, hope and charity house; it had one room on each floor. Built by John Hall and his wife Isabel, probably between 1771 and 1774, the house was described in an insurance policy issued by the Philadelphia Contributionship in 1774:

The house has a sixteen foot front, is twenty foot deep, two and half stories high with nine inch walls, plaster partitions, chimney breasts, panelled chimney pieces (the same on each floor), surbase and skirting in both stories, garret plastered, outside painted. Kitchen twenty by eleven, two stories high. Cost of house 175 pounds, cost of kitchen 75 pounds.

Flooring, woodwork, eared paneling and H and L hinges on the second and third floors are original, making 330 South Third one of the best preserved elegant small houses of the period. The first-floor woodwork is a faithful copy of that on the second floor, while the flooring and small stair rail are relics from Chaulkley Hall, a handsome mansion destroyed some years ago. The house was restored by Robert Trump; when he acquired it the word LAUNDRY was written in faded red letters on the first-floor plateglass window, one of its former occupants having been a Chinese laundryman.

The house was purchased in 1778 by William Wister, who lived there until after the death of his father, John Wister, in 1789.

Wister house parlor, showing a set of Birch prints, two Queen Anne chairs and a Martha Washington chair.

William spent the summers with his brother, Daniel Wister, at Grumblethorpe, Germantown. The place remained Wister property until 1853, when it was sold to Edward Styles, a grocer. It is said that sea captains have also lived in the house. Mr. and Mrs. Joseph L. Eastwick purchased it in 1960 and now use it as their town house. Mrs. Eastwick, the former Suzanne Wister, is a direct descendant of Daniel Wister.

A modern kitchen and bathrooms have been added, but from the outside 330 South Third presents the appearance and charm of a little house in a fairy tale. Mrs. Eastwick has furnished the ground floor to span the earlier Wister ownership, 1778-1853. A small rush-bottom chair used by William Wister as a child stands by the living-room fireplace. Among the handsome pieces are an early Philadelphia Quaker highboy, an early gaming table, a rare Queen Anne mirror, an antique model of a British ship that sailed the Delaware in Colonial days, a set of sixteen Birch prints of Philadelphia in 1800, struck off in 1900, and a picture of the old Philadelphia waterfront. On the wall are two notes of Colonial currency, signed by William Wister in 1773; below them are a photostatic copy of a letter written to him by Benjamin Franklin, dated London 1766, and a brass die used in the family importing business before 1818.

On the second floor are beds and a bureau from the William Wister wing of Grumblethorpe, probably made by a local carpenter of timber grown on the place. The third floor contains a Saratoga trunk and a washstand of the 1850s.

There is a tiny garden with boxwood grown from slips from the original box at Grumblethorpe, and wistaria vine, named in honor of the family. When the family came from the Palatinate early in the eighteenth century, one brother spelled his name Wister and the other Wistar, and this difference in spelling persists within the family to this day.

In the Wister House cellar are arches in which was stored Barbados rum — or at least empty rum barrels, kept there for future sale to traders, the cellar space serving in lieu of a warehouse. The outside cellar entrance has no steps, but a ramp down which the barrels were rolled.

The house is open to the public only on certain scheduled house tours.

The Wister House

Wister house garden, made from tiny backyard, is edged with box and contains a wisteria and a small fountain.

Wister house fireplace is faced with Delft tiles. Note child's chair once used by original owner, William Wister.

The Wister House

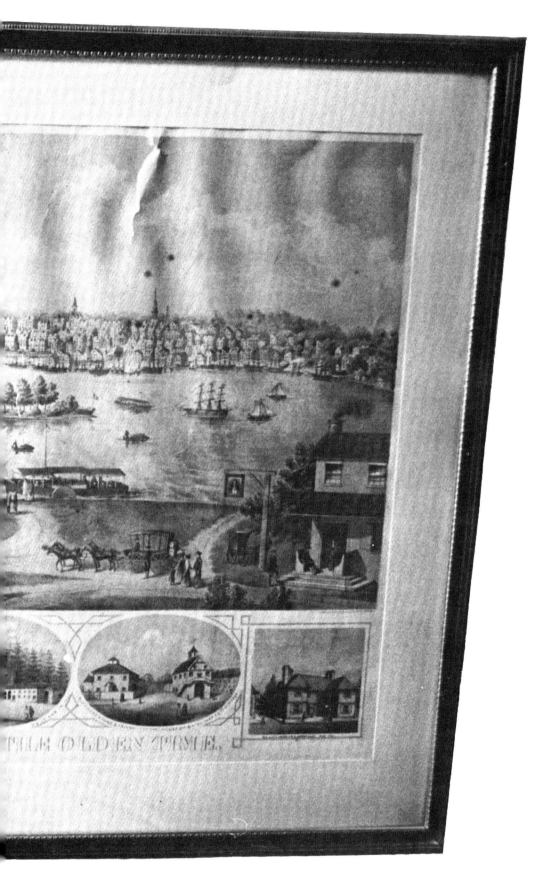

This print on the wall of the Wister house parlor shows Philadelphia and Society Hill as they looked in "the olden time."

The cellar at the Wister house, built with arches.

FIRE MARKS

Hand-in-Hand fire mark of the Philadelphia Contributionship

Fire marks are metal or wooden plaques which early fire-insurance companies placed on the fronts of houses they insured. The insurance-company brigades that preceded paid fire departments fought fires only in the houses on which their company insignia appeared.

The fire mark probably originated in London after the Great Fire of 1666. An insurance company called the Fire Office put up marks called Badges, painted in red or gold, about 1680. Some buildings bore several of them.

Fire marks or badges were first used in America in 1752, when the Philadelphia Contributionship for the Insurance of Houses from Loss by Fire started the practice. Its mark, the "Hand-in-Hand," four clasped hands made of lead and mounted on a wooden plaque, was originated by John Stow, who recast the Liberty Bell after it was cracked. The company also makes a mark entirely of metal.

The "Green Tree" — fire mark of the Mutual Assurance Company — was created when that company was founded in 1784 after the Contributionship decided not to insure houses

that were surrounded by trees. The Insurance Company of North America's first fire mark was a five-pointed star, and only two of them are in existence today; later it was changed to an eagle. The other well known fire mark — that of the Fire Association of Philadelphia — shows a fire plug between the letters F and A, with a section of hose on each side.

Fire marks are now used as antique decorations on houses not only in Society Hill but throughout Philadelphia. Many of the houses have actually been insured by one or another of these companies since they were built in the eighteenth or early nineteenth century.

The Insurance Company of North America has a set of 117 fire marks, some of them very rare. They can be seen at the company's main office, 16th and Arch streets.

Fire mark of the Fire Association (this picture, which does not show the familiar "F" on the left and "A" on the right, was furnished by the Reliance Insurance Company, successor of the Fire Association)

Eagle fire mark of the Insurance Company of North America

Green Tree fire mark of the Mutual Assurance Company

INDEX

Adam
  architecture, 119, 121
  mantelpiece, 68, 69
Adams, John, 114, 125
Alan, James, quoted, 98
Alexandria, Virginia, 167, 172
Alley, *see* Streets
altars, church, 147, 149, 152, 153, 155
American Daily Advertiser, quoted,
    53
American Philosophical Society, 110
"Andalusia," Biddle mansion, 125
andirons, French, 159
"Annals," by Watson, James F.,
    quoted, 81
Annenberg, Walter H., 57
Annenberg Fund, 57
arches
  brick, 13, 14, 15, 29, 30, 89, 135
  brick, marble-splayed, 43
  carved, 89, 90
  Greek Revival, 147
architects
  Brumbaugh, G. Edwin, 43, 55
  Cross, Edgar G., 2nd, 29
  Evans, David, Jr., 119
  Kearsley, John, 155
  Peterson, Charles E., 29, 159
  Roberts, George Brooke, 59, 165,
    167
  Smith, Robert, 155
  Strickland, William, 151
  Van Arkle and Moss, 69
  Walter, Thomas U., 125
architecture, periods and styles of
  Adam, 119, 121
  Colonial, 10, 11, 43, 57, 83, 98,
    107, 113, 119, 135, 147, 158,
    159, 165, 177, 179
  18th-century, 7, 9-15, 19, 43, 97,
    103, 113, 155, 165
  Empire, 23, 125
  Federal, 10, 11, 13, 35, 59, 87, 89

Georgian, 10, 35, 46, 87, 89, 135,
    154, 155, 165
Greek Revival, 10, 15, 113, 124,
    125, 133, 147, 150-51
architraves, 10, 57, 91, 135
archways, 61, 64, 69, 72, 135-36
armchairs, 159
  curly-maple, 128
  mahogany, Queen Anne, Savery,
    62-63
Athenaeum, The, 43
Ayer, N. W., 97, 98
Ayer, N. W. & Son, 97

Ballard, Ernesta Drinker, 46
balustrades, 23, 125
bar, inn, 81, 83, 84-85
Barclay, Alexander, 18, 19
Barclay House, 18-19
basement, 19, 21, 29, 30, 86, 89
  kitchens, 83, 91, 93, 132
bathrooms, 19, 21, 25, 29, 179
Batten, Harry A., 97
Bedford, Gunning, surveyor, 77
bedrooms, 21, 25, 73, 76, 81, 82, 83,
    97, 136, 146
  master, 19, 46, 50, 61, 63, 65, 69,
    160, 161
beds, four-poster, 82, 97
Bell, Robert, 21
Bell, William, 19
Bell's Court, 20-21
belt courses
  brick, 11, 45, 61, 110
  marble, 29, 43, 67, 135
Benjamin Franklin Clinic, 120
Biddle, Nicholas, 156
Biddle, Mrs. Peyton R., 123
Biddle mansion, "Andalusia," 125
Bingham, William, 23
Birch, prints by, 179

Bonaparte, Joseph, 156
Bond, Thomas, Dr., 120
Bouvier, Michel, 22, 23, 25
Bouvier Houses, 22-27
Bowen, Catherine Drinker, 46
Bracken, John P., 9
Bracken, Mrs. John P., 29
Bracken House, 28-33
brick
  arches, 13, 14, 15, 29, 30, 89, 135
  belt courses, 11, 45, 61, 110
  churches, 147, 151; 156
  "headers" and "stretchers," 11,
    97, 135
  houses, row, 9-16, 21, 29, 46, 61,
    94, 132-33, 177
  path, garden, 74
  "salmon," 11, 43
  walls, 9, 11, 14, 15, 74, 156
  water tables, 11
brickwork
  common bond, 11
  English bond, 11
  Flemish bond, 11, 29, 97, 110,
    119, 135, 159
Bristol Delft
  china, 83
  posset pots, 83
  tiles, 81, 82
Brockden, Charles, 46
Brockden, Richard, 46
brownstone-front houses, 9, 23
Brumbaugh, G. Edwin, 43, 55
Bucks County, Pennsylvania, 69
builders
  Cornell, John S., 43
  Davis, Samuel, 61
  Drinker, John, 46
  Grebe, Melvin H., 165
  Norris, Joseph Parker, Jr., 107
  Piles, John, 77
  Reynolds, John, 97, 98
  Reynolds, William, 97, 98